WALLACE STEVENS

A Spiritual Poet in a Secular Age

WALLACE STEVENS

A Spiritual Poet in a Secular Age

Charles M. Murphy

PAULIST PRESS
New York / Mahwah, N.J.

Frontispiece photo courtesy of The Huntington Library, San Marino, California.

The Publisher gratefully acknowledges use of excerpts from copyrighted works. From *The Complete Poems of Emily Dickinson.* Copyright 1976. Reprinted by permission of Little, Brown and Company. From *The Necessary Angel,* by Wallace Stevens. Copyright 1951 by Wallace Stevens. Reprinted by permission of Alfred A. Knopf, Inc. From *Collected Poems,* by Wallace Stevens. Copyright 1954 by Wallace Stevens. Reprinted by permission of Alfred A. Knopf, Inc. From *Opus Posthumous,* by Wallace Stevens. Copyright 1957 by Elsie Stevens and Holly Stevens. Reprinted by permission of Alfred A. Knopf, Inc. From *The Letters of Wallace Stevens,* edited by Holly Stevens. Copyright 1966 by Holly Stevens. Reprinted by permission of Alfred A. Knopf, Inc.

Cover design by Cynthia Dunne.

Library of Congress Cataloging-in-Publication Data

Murphy, Charles M.
    Wallace Stevens : a spiritual poet in a secular age / by Charles M. Murphy.
       p.   cm.
    Includes bibliographical references (p.   ).
    ISBN 0-8091-3708-9 (alk. paper)
    1. Stevens, Wallace, 1879-1995—Criticism and interpretation. 2. Spiritual life in literature. 3. Secularism in literature. I. Stevens, Wallace, 1879-1955. Poems. Selection. II. Title.
PS3537.T4753Z685 1997
811'.52—dc21
                                         96–51500
                                            CIP

Published by Paulist Press
997 Macarthur Boulevard
Mahwah, New Jersey 07430

Printed and bound in the United States of America

Contents

For C.M.M.
In memoriam

Children picking up our bones
Will never know that these were once
As quick as foxes on the hill...[1]

Sigla

CP   *The Collected Poems of Wallace Stevens. New York:* Alfred A. Knopf, 1954.

OP   *Wallace Stevens: Opus Posthumous Rev. ed. Edited by* Milton J. Bates. New York: Alfred A. Knopf, 1989.

NA   *The Necessary Angel: Essays on Reality and the Imagination.* New York: Vintage, 1951.

L   *The Letters of Wallace Stevens. Edited by* Holly Stevens. New York: Alfred A. Knopf, 1966.

Introduction

This is a study of Wallace Stevens and his unrelenting, lifelong search for God in the secular age in which we live. There was "never a more devout believer," Helen Vendler, one of his better interpreters has observed, "but a believer who shared the unbelief of his time."[2]

Stevens, who had a full career as a vice president of an insurance company, at the same time wrote the magnificent poetry that he said he needed to write. Poetry for him was no sideline; it was survival, an affair of the heart, a vital enterprise. He wrote his poems, he said, to "find God."[3] His aim was nothing less than to discover "how to live, what to do," in an age in which God for many people is more an absence than a presence.

Secularism is so pervasive that it is now considered normal in our culture. The public square is "naked" of God, and religion, a private option. People could conceivably live their entire lives without having an experience of the sacred that they can recognize. Some are satisfied with this condition. Wallace Stevens never was.

Stevens regarded his large poetic output, which became ever deeper, more masterly and inspired as he moved into old age, as a single body of work, a single poem, "part," he wrote, "of the never-ending meditation"[4] which was his life. "This endlessly elaborating poem," as he once described it, had as its purpose nothing less urgent than to evolve not just a theory of poetry but "the theory of life" itself,[5] an "amassing harmony."

In his solitary walks along the beach during vacations and daily to and from the office, Stevens meditated. From these meditations, his hard thinking, reading and observing, came the

1

poems. A world war was fought, elections were held, the stock market crashed, but these, to the dismay of his critics, did not invade his thoughts:

> He skips the journalism of subjects, seeks out
> The perquisites of sanctity, enjoys
>
> A strong mind in a weak neighborhood...[6]

What Stevens was after was a "fresh spiritual" in the particular circumstances of our time when religious symbols, even God, have become "an effulgence faded" because, he said with wit, "too venerably used."[7] He compared writing poetry to praying and the role of the poet to that of the priest. In a book of reflections which he kept and gave the title "Adagia," he confided:

> Wine and music are not good until afternoon. But poetry is like prayer in that it is most effective in solitude and in the times of solitude as, for example, in the earliest morning.[8]

"I write poetry," he said, "because it is part of my piety."[9]

By means of the poetry Stevens sought to enlarge life which he felt in this secular age had become dehumanized and diminished. Our existence he characterized as "poor," that is to say, deprived of imagination and nobility. Thus he wrote his poems not to impoverish it further by simply reflecting the prevailing skepticism and rationalism, but rather to enrich it and liberate it from these strictures.

In a volume of his poems that I cherish because of the personal inscription Stevens wrote inside to a colleague at the insurance company, Stevens, with typical bold strokes of the pen, in a few words said everything about himself and his intended audience:

> One is bound to write poetry for the highest values one is capable of and for the keenest spirits.

Among the three greatest poets America has produced, Walt Whitman, Emily Dickinson and Wallace Stevens, Stevens is by common consent the major spiritual writer. Going beyond the United States to the world context, Harold Bloom claims that "Stevens is the authentic twentieth-century poet of the Sublime, surpassing even Rilke in that highest of modes."[10] Stevens' serene last poems are, according to the British critic Frank Kermode, "the greatest modern poems in English about death and old age, and possibly about anything."[11]

The Approach We Shall Take: Stevens' Spirituality

Wallace Stevens has been studied in the forty years since his death from a variety of angles and viewpoints. As one critic, Joseph Riddel, observed, "Stevens is an exceptional instance among American modernists in being the poet who has served as an exemplary model for almost every mode and theory of literary criticism from the 1950's to the present, even when these theories were sharply contradictory and mutually exclusionary."[12] Stevens has obviously been examined from a literary standpoint. But there have also been other studies exploring his philosophy, his religious beliefs and even his contribution to the study of law (which is not so far-fetched since Stevens prided himself on being a practicing lawyer as well as a poet).[13] Ours is a study of the spiritual journey manifested in his poetry, a struggle that emerged out of his awareness of an absence at the heart of reality. Even with this terrible knowledge, Stevens strove mightily, and in the end achieved the ability to say "yes" to existence.

A person's spirituality is a most elusive thing. The deepest concerns of our hearts may escape even the most scrupulous biographer and most caring friend. But in the case of Stevens we have the poems, a unique and privileged access. They provide an astounding record of spiritual striving by a person in tune not only with himself, but also with the greatest expressions of culture in this century, the worlds of literature, art and philosophy. They are the poems "of our climate," the culture in which we live.

It was the critic Mark Van Doren who first spoke of Stevens' poetry as "a remarkable spiritual autobiography."[14] It is precisely this aspect of the poems that we shall explore. This, in fact, was the way Stevens conceived his role as poet. "The major poetic idea in the world is and always has been the idea of God," he wrote to his friend Henry Church. "The figures of the essential poets should be spiritual figures." But this "essential" task that Stevens set for himself was not easy, for, as he astutely observed: "One of the visible movements of the modern imagination is the movement away from God."[15]

The routines of the office were, in their own way, a relief from the hard spiritual work of poetry. "After I have walked home when I would ordinarily have a glass of water and a few cookies and sit down in an easy chair with the evening paper," Stevens wrote, "I go upstairs nowadays and work over my chore like one of the holy fathers working over his prayers."[16]

Writing as I do in prose about a poet is a humbling exercise. We stand before a master of language with our pedestrian explications. The poetry is the revelation. Our purpose can only be to lead back to the poems so that the very words of the poet can be experienced in all their power. For this reason, the poems we will be discussing are given in full in the concluding section of this book for easy reference.

We feel him nonetheless watching over our shoulder.

Question Reality

Belief in God requires a certain imagination according to Stevens. You have to pass beyond what human reason can demonstrate clearly and distinctly in order to discover the subtlety, the delicate shadings and shadows in which divinity dwells. You also, in order to encounter God, must shatter what is perceived to be the "facts" of our self-enclosed world and become awestruck by the higher and greater order which our daily routine obscures. To believe in God, Wallace Stevens claims, you have to question what passes for reality.

The particular way Stevens chose to develop his poetry was in terms of what he called "my reality and imagination complex." "Reality" refers to our everyday existence which in fact is a form of unreality. It's not merely that we tend to live only on the surface and attend only to appearances; it's rather the bigger and far more difficult problem of breaking out of a purely human-centered way of thinking. We fail to grasp in our self-enclosed world that the universe does not center itself upon us and our concerns. We need a fresh perspective: this is what Stevens calls imagination.

Imagination, he says, is like a walk in space, something that lifts us up to see life freshly. It allows us to discard old definitions of things thoughtlessly accepted, "the rotted names," he calls them. We all need to confront the question:

You as you are? You are yourself.[17]

But who is that self? This is not easily answered.

Here is where imagination can be the way to develop a spiritual life. Imagination is another word for sensibility, an acquired way of feeling and connecting, an ability to perceive and to interact, to make vital contact. Imagination, then, is a state of soul. It tells us that things are always more than they seem, only we have to be shaken up in order to realize it.

Poetry becomes the vehicle of imagination in introducing us to reality itself and not to some self-contrived version of it. Poetry does this by making us see things in a way we never have. Its images are often baffling, as Stevens himself once admitted.[18] Once we begin to understand that life always has this double quality of outer appearance and spiritual meaning, we are able to enter into that spiritual perspective which is the key to understanding Wallace Stevens' poetry.

But "baffling" is not an inappropriate way to describe this poetry. Examples abound.

Fairfield Porter was a painter who admired Stevens' poetry very much. Porter even painted a picture with Stevens' *Opus Posthumous* on the breakfast table. His wife, Anne, once recalled that upon going to bed one evening Porter clutched a volume of Stevens and was heard to murmur, "I'm going to understand them if it kills me!" a sentiment, alas, shared by many.

One of my own friends who is interested in all things religious acquired on my recommendation Stevens' *Collected Poems*.

Perusing the book's index, she came across the title "Arrival at the Waldorf." Having spent the early part of her life in New York City, she thought this might be a good place to begin. What she soon discovered, however, was that the "arrival" Stevens was concerned about in the poem had little to do with the Waldorf-Astoria Hotel on Park Avenue that she was familiar with. The hotel was merely the starting point for the poet's meditations, which had to do with "This arrival in the wild country of the soul."[19] Her hope-filled first encounter was thus completely thwarted.

Peter Brazeau in his oral biography of Stevens recounts an anecdote that came out of the office where Stevens worked. A colleague of many years finally got up the courage to tell the boss, "Mr. Stevens, I just can't understand your stuff. If I had to choose between you and Robert Service, I'd take Robert Service because I can understand Robert Service." (Service was the author of once-popular Western ballads.) Stevens replied, "Charlie, it isn't necessary that you understand my poetry. I understand it; that's all that's necessary."[20]

Although Stevens was known for this kind of dismissive remark, he nonetheless considered it part of his high vocation as a poet to perform a public function for society. The baffling quality of his writing has more to do with the subtle and elusive spiritual dimension of life that he was striving to communicate in verse.

Riding the New York City subways to a symposium on Stevens and modern art, I looked up to see to my surprise among the advertisements some lines from the Stevens' poem "Thirteen Ways of Looking at a Blackbird." The ad was part of a series on the subways entitled "Poetry in Motion." It amused me to think of the subway clientele trying to decipher Stevens' strange blackbird. The "thirteen ways" actually are not ways of looking but rather of evoking various sensations and states of the soul.

The Aim of This Study

Wallace Stevens is not alone in his spiritual predicament. There are many like him who have grown up in traditional religious homes and found themselves in adulthood wondering what that was all about and what it can mean to them now. Like Stevens also, but perhaps not to such a degree, many have come to appreciate the achievements of modern life and culture but find it difficult to integrate their secular knowledge with their inherited religious beliefs. Unlike Stevens, some have chosen simply to live a kind of two-level existence or to abandon religious practice altogether.

There are very many people who, because of the pressure of daily living, have no inner life to speak of.

To all these people Wallace Stevens has much to say. It is to make his rich spiritual insights available to a wider audience than literary scholars that I write this book.

In writing once to his daughter who at that time was planning to leave college and look for a job, Stevens advised, "But take my word for it, that making your living is a waste of time. None of the great things in life have anything to do with making your living."[21] How Stevens managed to cultivate a rich inner life and live his life on a reflective plane that transcended office and domestic routines makes him very relevant to us. This book aims to explore this contribution.

The desire for God never left him, so he had constantly as an adult to rethink who God is. What he discovered as he continued, as he said, "to widen my range," was that God became an even greater Reality than he ever imagined, more elusive and mysterious, but at the same time all the more central. We will see how this was so.

In his spiritual progress, Stevens began later in life to return to his Christian and ancestral roots. Earlier he had subjected them to withering critique but was learning to feel closer to them. Stevens once described a paradigm of the spiritual life which to an extent applied to himself. A person may begin life perhaps with a naive romanticism which often cannot survive later experience. Then a certain realism takes its place which can easily become fatalism and ultimately, indifference. But then, if we persist, we may find ourselves recommencing the cycle with what Stevens called a new romanticism, an enlarged vision of life now more confidently possessed.[22] What Stevens calls "a new romanticism" others would describe as adult faith. It should be added that while, according to this paradigm, these "stages" are said to be successive, they actually coexisted with one another in Stevens all his life. This fact makes it possible for commentators to stress one or another element in his poetry and to come to very different conclusions. In this way, too, Stevens is not untypical of the life of faith where faith and doubt are never far apart.

There are, among other notable interpreters of Stevens' religious views, Adalaide Kirby Morris' *Imagination and Faith* and the more recent *Wallace Stevens and the Question of Belief* by David Jarraway.[23] Morris argues that Stevens actually intended to substitute poetry for religion and the place of God. Jarraway does not agree that a close reading of Stevens would yield such a simple interpretation; he would say that Stevens was more interested in exploring his own mind and soul than in trying to explore ultimate reality. But neither Morris nor Jarraway can explain what has been frequently noted about Stevens: his "overanxiousness," as it has been called, about the question of religion and Christianity in particular.[24]

Morris makes use, in her presentation of Stevens' complex inner life, of something he wrote in 1951 in an essay entitled "Two or Three Ideas":

In an age of disbelief, or, what is the same thing, in a time that is largely humanistic, in one sense or another, it is for the poet to supply the satisfactions of belief, in his measure and in his style.[25]

It is true that Stevens assigns to the poet in the secular world a spiritual role, but he quickly adds the disclaimer "in his measure and in his style." Artistic creations can supply something of the "satisfactions" of belief but, according to Stevens, they do not and cannot substitute for God.

I agree with the reviewer of Jarraway's study who commented "David Jarraway in *Wallace Stevens and the Question of Belief* means to say, but, for some reason, is not quite up to saying, that Wallace Stevens' much-assumed anti-Christianity is really a form of anti-anti-Christianity."[26] I would say it is that, and more than that: Stevens is making a plea, or better, an actual attempt, to have Christian beliefs become more clearly related to the actual world in which we live.

Wallace Stevens was no dilettante in the realm of the spirit. With great discipline and dedication he devoted himself to his double love: the love of heaven and the love of earth. His was an ardent suitor's devotion to them both, even when these two loves seemed incompatible with one another in a luminous harmony.

Wallace Stevens would resonate with the challenge St. Teresa of Avila issued in her *Interior Castle:*

> It is no small pity and should cause us no little shame that, through our own fault, we do not understand ourselves or know who we are. Would it not be a sign of great ignorance if a person were asked who he was and could not say?[27]

The Two Ways

The poetry of Stevens evolved in two phases. It is significant, I believe, that they correspond to the two traditional ways in Catholic theology whereby human beings can encounter the reality of God apart from divine revelation. The poetry of the first phase concentrates with gusto upon the physical world we inhabit and our terrestrial existence with all its tragic beauty. The later poems are a departure, more introspective, the poet confronting himself and his unfulfilled desires.

In the psalms of the Bible we read, "The heavens declare the glory of God and the vault of heaven proclaims his handiwork."[28] By pondering the marvels of creation, a way is made available to people who do not have the biblical revelation in words and sacred history to encounter the divine. Similarly, every person, whether consciously religious or not, has an inner life, a personal freedom, a sense of moral goodness, a longing for the infinite which nothing finite can satisfy. The inner life of the spirit likewise can open up to God.[29] But what if, after

Charles Darwin and his *Origin of Species,* the world cannot easily be perceived as a divine creation but appears more as a still-evolving product of chance, "unsponsored" and "free"? And, what if the longings of your heart do not seem to correspond to any religious conceptions you know of? This, oversimply stated, was Stevens' spiritual predicament. The two traditional routes to God have become blocked, for him and many others.

Upon accepting the National Book Award for his poetry near the end of his life, Stevens once again alluded to these newly different perceptions of our earthly and personal existence, and to the now unquestioned assumptions whereby we live in this secular age. "After all," he commented, "one must live in the world of Darwin and not of Plato."[30] Darwin seemed to have swept away any illusions we might have had about ourselves as the center of the universe and the universe itself as being transparent of divine purpose. Whatever grandeur, nobility and order our existence may have, Stevens asserts many times, and with typical rigor and integrity, must somehow be "discovered" anew but never "imposed," in order to be credible.

How Wallace Stevens negotiated these two ways to God may be of immense help to many who are trying to walk the same paths.

After giving a sketch of the life of the poet, I will devote the separate chapters to the early poetry of the earth and then to the later, soaring poetry of the soul. In concluding chapters, I will explore how helpful Stevens may be to people today in their own spiritual lives and express an appreciation of his work from the point of view of Catholic theology.

A Spirituality for Today

The last thing in the world Wallace Stevens wanted was to be called a mystic. Such a label carries with it connotations of special experiences as well as of mystification. When Stevens sat by the window and meditated while looking out, he did so in order to become part of what he saw, to become part of the real. Nonetheless, he and the great Spanish mystic St. Teresa have much in common. Teresa lived in the sixteenth century and

Stevens in the twentieth, but both experienced the same kind of spiritual loss when conventional religion loses its fervor. Both, by the labor of communicating their spiritual experiences, strove to awaken a new awareness in their contemporaries when the old formulas had grown weak.

The aim of mystical prayer or meditation for both St. Teresa and for Wallace Stevens is the same: it is, as Stevens puts it, that "the world is no longer an extraneous object, full of other extraneous objects, but an image. In the last analysis, it is with this image of the world that we are vitally concerned."[31] Meditation, then, is not just "thinking." St. Francis de Sales explained the difference: meditation does involve thought, he said, but thought lifted up to a noble plane in order to arouse in us the deepest of emotions. It is to be "vitally concerned."[32]

There is, however, a most significant way in which Stevens and St. Teresa are in contrast, a way which is a significant departure from the mystical tradition from which she comes. Teresa regards the Earth and all that it contained, including the human body, to be a heavy burden to her, one that prevents her soul from taking flight to God. For her, the divine and earthly realms are simply opposed to one another. "Bodily existence is a constant counterweight to mystical experience," she wrote. Stevens would put it another way. What Teresa identifies as physical or material, Stevens would describe as our surface, human-centered perception. Most emphatically he rejects the notion that our physical nature in itself has no spiritual meaning or is an obstacle in our spiritual lives. In fact, according to Stevens, no account of the spiritual life is valid which leaves out the physical side of life.

Here, I believe, Stevens makes his most significant contribution to our present spiritual situation. To be believable, spirituality must be rooted in the earth to which we belong. Stevens put it this way: "The poet is the intermediary between people and the world in which they live and also, between people as between themselves, but not between people and some other world."[33]

> I am a native of this world
> And I think in it as a native thinks.[34]

In these lines from "The Man with the Blue Guitar" Stevens expresses the need for a spirituality which we would term incarnational, one that is sacramental—the earth itself suffused with spiritual significance:

the flesh, the bone, the dirt, the stone.[35]

It is a sanctity of ordinary life, one that encompasses, as Stevens says, the fruit and wine, the book and bread, things as they are.[36] What one longs for, he declares in this same poem, is to discover "a missal in the mud"[37]: a whole text, or even a page of a text or at least a phrase that relates to life as we have to live it every day.

This is a spirituality not just confined to Sunday, but one suited for all the Mondays of our lives.[38] "An Ordinary Evening in New Haven" is the subject of one of his greatest meditations, with emphasis on the *ordinary*.

The Goal of the Spiritual Life: Total Grandeur

One hot summer afternoon in Rome, where I was studying for the priesthood, a fellow seminarian and his mother joined me for a picnic lunch in the Roman Forum. Between bits of bread and cheese we read Wallace Stevens. The poem we read, passing the book around, was "The Man with the Blue Guitar," a work occasioned by a painting by Picasso. As we continued to read to each other I realized that as I sat upon the ground I was being bitten by ants. I tried to ignore them. This pedestrian intrusion upon such a noble scene was actually very Stevens-like. Hadn't he mischievously entitled poems "St. John and the Backache" and "The Worms at Heaven's Gate"?

Not far from us in these famous imperial ruins was the Blue Nuns' Hospital on the Celian Hill run by the Little Company of Mary, a religious congregation from Ireland. It was well known to us seminarians, and some of the nuns were our friends. In this hospital, eight years before, in 1952, the philosopher George Santayana had died at the age of eighty-nine. It was Professor

Santayana at Harvard who had introduced Wallace Stevens to the larger world of religious imagination. Their friendship extended to the exchange of poems. Ever the genteel critic of American life, Santayana, a Catholic in all but faith, acquainted students with the symbolisms and ecstasies of the great religious mystics. Stevens was enthralled.

Later in life Stevens would fault Santayana for his lack of seriousness that excluded him from the rank of the truly great philosophers, but very near the end of his own life Stevens wrote a compassionate tribute to a guiding influence. That poem, "To an Old Philosopher in Rome," may serve as an excellent summation of Wallace Stevens' spiritual goal, for it fits the author more than the purported subject.

The tone of "To an Old Philosopher in Rome" is majestic. Its mood is one of eternity and fulfillment in the contemplation of life's end. It represents a point of arrival and achievement. The one who earlier "raged against chaos" and who is a self-described "inquisitor of structures" stops at the threshold of heaven and rejoices that the design of all his words "takes form...and is realized." Mercy, absolution, a hovering excellence—these are the terms employed to describe the scene in the hospital room.

As I now reread "To an Old Philosopher in Rome," I contrast it and its spiritual achievement with Emily Dickinson's poem of similar theme, "Because I Could Not Stop for Death." Dickinson too had her doubts about the Christian creed, but her portrayal of eternal life in the poem is quite different from that of Stevens; it is much less believable because it is still tied to an old mythology.

Like Dickinson, Stevens sees "the majestic movement / Of men growing small in the distance of space, / Singing, with smaller and still smaller sound." The vehicle to eternity, however, in the Dickinson poem is a celestial chariot bearing away Death and Immortality as well as herself. The chariot rises from the earth; a house becomes "a swelling of the ground," its roof "scarcely visible." Dickinson concludes:

> Since then—'tis Centuries—and yet
> Feels shorter than the Day

> I first surmised the Horses' Heads
> Were toward Eternity—[39]

For Stevens celestial chariots are nothing more than "dear gorgeous nonsense."[40] What Stevens offers in their place represents the hard-won fruit of his lifelong poetic search and ultimate faith. His is a vision of eternity which is tied to earth and continuous with it. Eternal life itself is not vacant: "The life of the city never lets go, nor do you / Ever want it to." Everything we are familiar with has become enlarged and yet remains no more than itself. This is a totally "human end" though more than human: "Not of its sphere, and yet not far beyond," "in the spirit's greatest reach." The actual city becomes the image and symbol of that for which it is the threshold, "that more merciful Rome beyond," "the two alike."

Here clearly stated is the poet's recapturing of basic Christian belief about the ultimate destiny of our planetary life. The earth, though miserable and poor, is destined for glorious transformation, a transformation which pertains not merely to souls in some other realm but to the body, the complete person, the contents of the world. To illustrate this, Stevens uses the striking image of two parallel lines which in perspective become one so that "Men are part of both in the inch and in the mile"; he speaks of "banners blowing which are with ease transformed into wings."

Thus, in the final years of his life when "To an Old Philosopher in Rome" was written, Wallace Stevens discovered the greatest happiness and fulfillment. He had been able to express for the sake of himself and others the loftiest things; he unveiled for the world the majesty which the bird-nested and rain-stained arches and vaults of the church have allowed to become obscure. Like Teresa, he had built his own interior castle, untouched by any bitterness or regret, a place for God to dwell in.

I want to thank particularly the following persons who aided me in my meditations upon Wallace Stevens' questions: Gerald O'Collins, S.J. and John Michael McDermott, S.J., of the Gregorian University; Jasper Hopkins of the University of

Minnesota; Milton J. Bates of Marquette University and Avery Dulles, S.J. of Fordham University.

Finally, I want to express my thanks to the North American College in Rome whose hospitality and assistance I enjoyed during the writing of a portion of this book.

Memoriam and Introduction

[1] "A Postcard from the Volcano," in CP, 158.

[2] Helen Vendler, *Wallace Stevens: Words Chosen Out of Desire* (Knoxville: University of Tennessee, 1984) 40.

[3] "The Irrational Element in Poetry" (essay), in OP, 227.

[4] "An Ordinary Evening in New Haven," in CP, 465.

[5] Ibid., CP, 486.

[6] Ibid., CP, 474.

[7] "Notes toward a Supreme Fiction," in CP, 400.

[8] "Adagia," in OP, 189.

[9] L, 478.

[10] Harold Bloom, *Poetry and Repression: Revisionism from Blake to Stevens* (New Haven: Yale, 1976) 282.

[11] Frank Kermode, *Wallace Stevens* (London: Faber and Faber, 1989) xiv.

[12] Joseph Riddel, *The Clairvoyant Eye: The Poetry and Poetics of Wallace Stevens* (Baton Rouge: Louisiana State, 1991) xiii.

[13] Thomas C. Grey, *The Wallace Stevens Case: Law and the Practice of Poetry* (Cambridge: Harvard, 1991).

[14] Joan Richardson, *Wallace Stevens: A Biography. The Later Years: 1923–1955* (New York: William Morrow, 1988) 26–27.

[15] L, 378.

[16] L, 579.

[17] "The Man with the Blue Guitar, " in CP, 183.

[18] L, 302.

[19] "Arrival at the Waldorf," in CP, 240.

[20] Peter Brazeau, *Parts of a World: Wallace Stevens Remembered. An Oral Biography* (New York: Random House, 1983) 43–44.

[21] L, 426.

[22] L, 350.

[23] Adalaide Kirby Morris, *Wallace Stevens: Imagination and Faith* (Princeton: Princeton University, 1974). David R. Jarraway, *Wallace Stevens and the Question of Belief: Metaphysician in the Dark* (Baton Rouge: Louisiana State, 1993).

[24] See Richard Poirier, *Poetry and Pragmatism* (Cambridge: Harvard, 1992) 158.

[25] "Two or Three Ideas" (essay), in OP, 259.

[26] Alan Filreis, *The Wallace Stevens Journal* 17 (Fall 1993): 251.

[27] St. Teresa of Avila, *Interior Castle,* trans., E. Allison Peers (New York: Doubleday Image, 1989) 29.

[28] Psalm 19:1.

[29] See *The Catechism of the Catholic Church* (Washington, D.C.: United States Catholic Conference, 1994) 14–16.

[30] Remarks on receiving the National Book Award for Poetry, in OP, 289.

[31] "Imagination as Value" (essay), in NA 151.

[32] Louis Martz highlights elements of Ignatian meditation techniques in Stevens' poetry. See "The World as Meditation," in *Literature and Belief,* ed. M.H. Abrams (New Haven: Yale, 1958) 157.

[33] "Adagia," in OP, 189. For an exposition of the relation between poetry and prayer, see Stevens' essay, "The Irrational Element in Poetry," OP 221–23.

[34] "The Man with the Blue Guitar," in CP, 180.

[35] Ibid., CP, 176.

[36] Ibid., CP, 172.

[37] Ibid., CP, 177.

[38] Ibid., CP, 183.

[39] Emily Dickinson, *The Complete Poems,* ed. Thomas Johnson, (Boston: Little Brown, 1960) 350.

[40] "The Noble Rider and the Sound of Words" (essay), in NA, 3.

Part One

1

Nomad Exquisite:
The Life of the Poet as Spiritual Figure

Wallace Stevens led a nomadic life, wide-ranging and forever exploratory of unknown lands and exotic destinations. All these significant journeys were within.

Born in Pennsylvania, educated at Harvard, living and working for a time in New York City and finally settling in Hartford, Connecticut, he traveled little in the usual sense. Regular vacation trips to Florida, some business trips, forays into New York City—that's about all there was. His wife was not a good traveler, but this could not have been the principal reason why France, the land of his dreams, remained forever only a place from which he received welcome postcards. His was "a spirit without foyer in this world."[1] His lifelong pilgrimage was spiritual.

In a rare self-disclosure, Stevens once confided, "Life is an affair of people, not of places. But for me it is an affair of places and that is the trouble."[2] But the places were principally of the imagination. Shy and diffident by nature, his principal energies increasingly over the years went into the "meditative ecstasies of apprehension" that Harold Bloom speaks about when he describes the uneventfulness of Stevens' exterior life:

> In our time, among writers of the first order, only the life
> of Wallace Stevens seems as lackluster in outward event or
> excitement as Shakespeare's. We know that Stevens hated
> the graduated income tax and that Shakespeare was quick
> to bring suits to Chancery to protect his estate invest-
> ments. We know, more or less, that neither Shakespeare's

21

nor Stevens' marriage was particularly passionate, once past its origin. After that we work at knowing the plays, or at knowing Stevens' intricate variations on his meditative ecstasies of apprehension.[3]

Florida, for Stevens, was not merely a welcome respite from the rigors of Connecticut but became an imaginative construct, a place of nature's exuberance. But eventually Stevens gave up this annual ritual of vacations in Key West as his spiritual journey progressed in an ever more homeward direction. In the poem, "Farewell to Florida," he sails from "her home, not mine" to "My North," though it be "leafless and lies in a wintry slime."[4] That journey ultimately will bring him back even further to his ancestral roots, to the ghostly, luminous presences of his religious forebears[5] and "The Old Lutheran Bells at Home."[6]

Like his father, Wallace Stevens was an intimidating physical presence, over six feet tall and weighing over two hundred pounds. A shy man, who at the same time enjoyed conviviality, he covered over his unease with a diffident, cold manner and his self-doubt with a series of poetic disguises. Cherishing solitude and enamored of candlelight, he found his artistic voice within the impulse of modernism by which he sought to create expressions appropriate to his time and for the people of his time and not merely for himself. Stevens was a man of great seriousness and idealism who often was mistaken in his writings for a fop, a sensualist, someone overly proud of his sardonic wit.

There is ample evidence of his social awkwardness and insensitivity, but even with his closely guarded privacy his compassion could be seen. He carried on extended correspondences with younger artists and even the inquiring nun. He underwent agonies of remorse if he ever offended anyone who was a friend. But, most of all, it was his fidelity to Elsie, his wife, that impressed people. Others, like their daughter Holly, may have commented upon her "persecution complex"[7] and he himself in his poetry could make reference to "the hating woman," the one who "turns cold at his light touch,"[8] but Stevens kept a perfect silence and maintained their relationship until his death.

Stevens' basic spiritual search came down to this: to construct himself, to find himself through poetry in the masculine world where poetry was somehow unmanly and in the artistic milieu of modernism where religious ideas were unacceptable; to create a mythology of self while seeking and needing a mythology of the world itself to base himself upon.

The World as Insurance Executive

For all his concentration upon poetry, and even after the acclaim which he began to receive for it, Wallace Stevens chose not to retire from the Hartford Accident and Indemnity Company where he processed surety claims from 1916 until his death. In *Who's Who in America,* Stevens listed his profession as "insurance." His promotion in 1934 to vice president of the firm was a matter of great pride.

According to Richard Eberhart, a younger poet whom Stevens befriended, "He lived in a world of grand Republicanism, of big houses, of wanting to make a large salary and of living with noble people."[9] In not very complimentary fashion, he was referred to as "the man in the four piece suit," shoes impeccably shined, only newly printed bills in his wallet, "John D. Rockefeller drenched in attar of roses."[10] He could swap sexist stories with male companions over several martinis at the Canoe Club, sharing common prejudices.

"Making it" in that world evidently meant much to the young man whom his father pegged an impractical dreamer. A vivid impression of him at the age of thirty-six is supplied by Harriet Monroe, an early editor and encourager of his poetry:

> Have you ever known Stevens? He's a big, slightly fat, awfully competent looking man. You expect him to roar, but when he speaks there emerges the gravest, softest, most subtly modulated voice I've ever heard—a voice on tiptoe at dawn.[11]

In a revelatory aside in the "Adagia," among the many definitions of poetry, Stevens writes, "Money is a kind of poetry."[12]

Among his assistants in the marbled halls of executive row at the Hartford was John Ladish who came to work there in 1924, the year of the birth of Stevens' only daughter, Holly Bright Stevens. He and Arthur Sigmans were the only Catholics working in this anti-Catholic environment. In my interviews with John Ladish's son, Father Robert Ladish, he recalled that his father was told he should join the Masons as a way of future promotion. Ladish instead started wearing his Knights of Columbus pin to work. He was never promoted.

John Ladish was trusted enough by Stevens to be given the keys to his house whenever Stevens was away. Among the personal recollections of Stevens preserved in Peter Brazeau's oral biography, Ladish's were among the more charitable. "When that book came out," Father Ladish recalled, "we howled with laughter over the things people said about Wallace." A story which John Ladish chose not to retell in the book was one his wife used often to repeat, it must have hurt her so. "When my parents were first married," Father Ladish said in his telling of the tale which had entered his family's folklore, "they lived in the southern end of Hartford. They saved and saved for the day when they would own a home of their own. The crash of 1929 delayed their plans, but in 1936 they had built their new home in West Hartford. It was a modest four-bedroom house next door to the Sigmans. My father wanted his boss to come to see the new house. It was on that occasion that Mr. Stevens said something my mother never forgot. Upon entering he said, 'Isn't it grand that people like you can own a house like this!'"[13]

Although Wallace Stevens was indomitable at the office, he seemed less commanding in his private life. Elsie was a woman whose striking good looks inspired an artist living in the same apartment building as the Stevens' in New York City to use her face as the model for the famous Liberty Walking half dollar and the Mercury dime. This information Wallace Stevens rarely divulged. Though an excellent cook and gardener, the untutored Elsie had reservations about her husband's poetry: "He writes so much that is affected," she once said.[14]

Much has been said about their reclusive life. Was it Elsie's reputed mental illness or the poet's own temperament? Stories abound.

Alfred A. Knopf, his publisher, arriving from New York City to discuss a new volume of poetry, was kept on the front lawn for their conversation. He never knew why. Once Governor Abraham Ribicoff stopped his limousine to offer Stevens a ride. Stevens accepted but said nothing until, upon arriving at his destination, said, "Do not think because I have accepted your offer of a ride we are to become social friends." Ribicoff liked to tell this one on himself. Neighbors on Westerly Terrace noted that children playing with a ball in the yard next to Stevens' occasionally sent a ball over the fence into Stevens' property. The ball was never returned.

Stevens away from home retained his comic side. "Have You Ever Seen a Dream Walking?" was reported to be a favorite request of his in New York night clubs. Business associates sometimes were treated to his favorite cinnamon buns before getting down to business. A neighbor once brought him a piece of pie. "Mr. Stevens," she gushed, "this is called Heavenly Pie." The poet exclaimed, "Open up the gates!"

The Hartford Courant for Sunday, August 1, 1993, near the thirty-eighth anniversary of Wallace Stevens' death, published a reminiscence by a former insurance colleague under the title, "Poet in Pinstripes." In person, Stevens was physically imposing, but more impressive, it was recalled, was his "deep, ingrained sense of privacy." Several anecdotes were recounted to make this point, among which was the following:

> When I arrived at the home office in 1950, fresh from the West, I was given an introductory tour. I was told that I would do well not to insult Stevens' intellect with trivial or mundane conversation.
>
> And so it was that when our habits brought us to the executive washroom at identical times, I took pains simply to acknowledge his presence. He did mine and nothing more. This went on for some time until one morning he turned to me and asked in his resonant baritone for a word with me. I recoiled, wondering what gaffe I had committed.

He went on, "You and I have been meeting in this sanctum
for many months and you have said to me, 'Good morning,
Mr. Stevens,' and I have said, 'Good morning, Mr. Lange,'
and with that we have each gone our own way. You have
not commented on the weather nor the latest political
fiasco nor some sporting outcome—and for that I wish to
thank you."[15]

The Walking Man

In the later phase of his life, after the long lapse which followed the publication of his first volume of poems, *Harmonium,*
in 1923, which had received such a disappointing reception,
Stevens found a new way of composing verse: walking to work.[16]
Walking was always an important part of Stevens' life from his
earliest days. The countryside around Reading, Pennsylvania,
was within walking distance, and even during his New York
years Stevens took delight in walking great distances outside the
city. In an early poem, "Of the Surface of Things," Stevens
wrote:

> In my room, the world is beyond my understanding;
> But when I walk I see that it consists of three or four
>   hills and a cloud.[17]

A picture of the poet emerges from lines in "Palace of the
Babies" written in 1921, two years after "Of the Surface of
Things":

> The walker in the moonlight walked alone.
> And in his heart his disbelief lay cold.
> His broad-brimmed hat came close upon his eyes.[18]

"Perhaps," Stevens wrote, "the truth depends on a walk around
the lake."[19]

The walking man walks because in fact he did not own an
automobile and never possessed a driver's license. But more, the
walking man walks because it is the pace of meditation. He

wishes to disclose "the actual landscape with its actual horns" in order to achieve "an essential integrity."[20]

Stevens' two-mile walks to work from 118 Westerly Terrace past Elizabeth Park to work took forty minutes and became occasions for poems. The walking influenced not only the cadences of the verse but also determined the aphoristic shape of his lines. A secretary transcribed his jottings once he arrived, a small way of beating the system he jokingly said.

A long-time neighbor of the Stevenses' was Florence Berkman, whose home was the former carriage house on the property of the mansion occupied by the governors of Connecticut. She recently published a reminiscence of the poet as he walked by her house:

> But perhaps our most distinguished neighbor was Hartford's world-renowned poet, Wallace Stevens. From 1942 to 1955, we were enriched by his presence. Promptly at 9 o'clock every morning I would see him walking down Terry Road on his way to the Hartford Fire and Indemnity Co., where he was a vice president.
>
> About that time in the morning I would be at my kitchen sink washing the breakfast dishes. This glimpse of a great poet gave a lift to my day. He was a tall, imposing figure and walked slowly and rhythmically, almost in cadences. About 4 in the afternoon I would see him walking home, often while I was walking Cappie, our cocker spaniel. He never greeted me, and did not even look at me. Later I learned that when he was creating his verses he was unaware of the activity around him.
>
> On Saturdays and Sundays, in sunshine and sleet, Stevens walked to Elizabeth Park. My husband was often out in front, weeding the lawn, and the poet would stop for a chat.
>
> But one rainy morning I was dashing out of the driveway on the way to the dentist. Stevens was standing on the corner of Terry Road and Asylum Road absolutely sopping. He had no umbrella.
>
> "Mr. Stevens," I asked, "would you like a lift?"

He said, "Oh, I would love it."

Since he had never acknowledged my existence I thought I would introduce myself. He replied, "I know who you are. You live in that little house. I often thought I would love to see the inside of your house."

"You are invited," I said.

On the ride downtown he talked at length. I then became aware that he had lovely, blue-violet eyes. He explained he was furious at the *New Statesman,* an English magazine that was very anti-American at the time. I asked him how he found the time to read so many periodicals. He said, "I get up every morning at 6 and read for two hours."

I was excited by my adventure and that night told my husband that Stevens was coming to call. He never came. He died in 1955, one year before my husband, who was to write the obituary of his friend and one of our great poets. Although Stevens came to the Hartford Fire in 1916, he was known in this community only as the vice president of a major insurance company. That he was a poet wasn't known but to a few friends.[21]

José Rodríguez Feo is an example of a younger poet whom Stevens befriended and encouraged. He recalled: "He (Stevens) always would emphasize when we talked that I had to think more. Once, in a letter he said, 'You have to think two or three hours everyday.' When we met he said, 'You have to think (not only) about what you read, but you have to think about your life and the things around you.'...In one of his letters he remarks, 'I...really read very much less of everything than most people. It is more interesting to sit round and look out the window.'"[22]

In an early letter written to his future wife, Stevens acknowledged that writing poetry was part of the process of defining himself. "It seems insincere," he said, "like playing a part, to be one person on paper and another in reality. But I know it is only because I command myself there."[23]

In the poems the two selves came together, the poet and the businessman. In the later poetry especially, the comedian of many disguises began to speak more freely in his own voice. Once the quiet observer, he could at last relinquish the harlequinade and confidently become one with the world.

"We felt, looking back," Father Ladish reflected concerning his own family of modest means and the life of his father's boss, "that we had immensely more than Mr. Stevens did. All he had, the poor man, were those few friends in New York City who knew his poetry and made a lot of him."

In August, 1991, as the rain fell in Hartford, I visited the grave of Wallace Stevens in Cedar Hill Cemetery at 453 Fairfield Avenue. I was coming from the funeral of the archbishop of Hartford, John Whealon, who succeeded Archbishop Henry O'Brien. It was O'Brien who, according to some accounts, instructed the chaplain of St. Francis Hospital—where Wallace Stevens died—not to make a public record of Stevens' deathbed baptism and conversion to Catholicism.

There was something almost comic about the cemetery office where I went to ask directions to the grave. The two secretaries carried out their pragmatic functions housed in a pseudo-Gothic stone structure nestled next to the cemetery's large ornamental gate; oddly, the cramped space seemed in keeping with the larger conception of the cemetery itself. The stately park and its plantings and pools make Cedar Hill a model of the Transcendentalist mythology of death and the cemetery as the threshold of eternity.

The name "Wallace Stevens" elicited no special recognition as the secretary searched for him in the files. She helpfully indicated his grave on a map: Section 14, five rows in.

His stone was modest. It bore only the names of him and his wife, Elsie Viola Kachel, their dates in Gothic letters: for him October 2, 1879, Reading, Pennsylvania and August 2, 1955, Hartford, Connecticut; for her, June 5, 1886, and February 19, 1963. There was no line of poetry. Two drooped lilies completed the surface. Although poets occupied a more significant place in society in the 1950's than they do today, the memorial to Stevens in no way compares with the magnificent mausoleum in the same cemetery of the business tycoon J.P. Morgan.

Dante Alighieri, the poet Wallace Stevens wished to surpass, was given dramatically greater honor in his city of Florence. Dante's memorial cenotaph stands in the national pantheon, the Church of Santa Croce, before which a statue of the poet dominates the square. Near the monument to Dante are the tombs of Michelangelo, Donatello, Raphael, Leonardo da Vinci and Galileo. Across the monument, beneath a seated, larger-than-life image of Dante, are the words: "Onorate l'altissimo' poeta." ("Honor the poet most sublime.")

In 1950, William Van O'Connor, a critic Stevens had encouraged, published *The Shaping Spirit: A Study of Wallace Stevens.* While Stevens appreciated the recognition, he was uncomfortable with the book's first chapter, "Stevens as Legend." It used the term "alienation" to describe the poet's stance toward his society. Stevens found that a difficult evaluation. O'Connor writes:

> There is nothing especially strange about a poet like Stevens dividing his life between insurance and poetry. Other poets also live in the middle-class world, as doctors or teachers or employees in publishing houses. They manage to live like Stevens with a foot in each world, but he, a great poet and successful insurance man, seems to dramatize in an ironic fashion the brink between the world of the poet and the world of business. Also the substance and manner of his poetry appear incongruous against the middle-class business world in which Stevens has lived.[24]

Yet Stevens himself in his meditative walks came to the same conclusion:

> I was the world in which I walked, and what I saw
> Or heard or felt came not but from myself;
> And there I found myself more truly and more strange.[25]

What amazes us now is the extent to which Stevens actually transcended his world, how he escaped the prejudices and patriotisms of his time and wrote a poetry of universal reference. And, most of all, we stand in awe of how he cultivated a life of such interiority and freshness of vision that he could triumph over the strictures of the pervasive secularist ideologies of our day.

The World as Meditation

As the years advanced, Wallace Stevens' world became more and more centered upon poetry: "the world as meditation." In the poem of that title, Stevens reflects upon these double worlds he now inhabits: the world of exteriors in which he carries out his duties at the Hartford Accident and Indemnity Company and at 118 Westerly Terrace, and simultaneously, the untamed, "savage" and "barbarous" world he encounters in his meditation, the world of his deepest desires.

The poem, "The World as Meditation," is introduced with an epigraph given in French from the violinist and composer Georges Enesco. In the reworking which Stevens makes of Enesco's words, Enesco is made to say that he has spent "too much time" travelling and playing his violin; Enesco, rather, refers to having spent "precious time" in these external pursuits. Enesco goes on to speak about the original and powerful creations that come from concentration, which Stevens renders, "The essential exercise of the composer, meditation, was never suspended in me." Stevens then heightens Enesco's statement "I carry within me a permanent dream" to "I am living a permanent dream, one that does not cease, by day or by night."[26]

The scene depicted in the poem, Penelope in a solitary reverie awaiting the return of Ulysses, could have come out of a painting by Edward Hopper. There are many concordances between Stevens' poetry and the world of music and painting. Paul Klee and Pablo Picasso are painters frequently mentioned. More recently Stevens has been compared with Hopper. As in a work by Hopper, a solitary female figure sits deep in thought combing her hair. The room is starkly lit. The figure, though ordinary, is identified as one from Greek mythology who in Homeric myth awaits the return of her lover from his far-flung journeys.

Both Hopper and Stevens came from similar conservative nineteenth-century American towns whose exterior calm and solidity they perceived to be engulfed by larger forces difficult to comprehend. Each one's technique, in its own way, is brilliant, but that brilliance conveys a similar vacancy in the center of existence, "a vision of the world without us: not merely a place that excludes us, but a place emptied to us."[27] Both place everyday life within mythic spaces and times, as if to say that what happens to us compared with what has gone on before and since is trivial; the narratives we construct for our lives appear merely sentimental and beside the point.

"The World as Meditation" does bear these similarities to Hopper but also reveals illuminating differences. The vivid contrast between light and darkness is there, but in Stevens the darkness is not menacing or a symbol of despair and the light is not cruel but warm, golden and comforting.

Concerning darkness, in another poem which is a longer meditative exercise, "An Ordinary Evening in New Haven," darkness is described:

> As of a long, inevitable sound,
> A kind of cozening and coaxing sound,
> And the goodness of lying in a maternal sound,
>
> Unfretted by day's separate, several selves,
> Being part of everything come together as one.[28]

Here the darkness is giving way to day and winter is receding into spring. Winter, the season in Stevens which is "a spiritual nothingness that discloses the divine absence,"[29] is passing and a presence which is Ulysses, or, rather, more than Ulysses, what Ulysses represents, is coming constantly so near. Ulysses, when he comes will hold no threat for he will be

> Companion to his self for her, which she imagined,
> Two in a deep-founded sheltering, friend and dear friend.[30]

The planet itself, whose mysterious renewal was "mending" the trees even as she muses, encourages her hopes. Her meditation therefore is "inhuman," that is to say, more than human, more than self-deception: one rather that is "essential," totally at one with reality. Stevens in "The World as Meditation" is not only doing an actual meditation but demonstrating how meditation is itself "the world."

Meditation, according to St. Francis de Sales, is not the same as thinking. Thinking, he explains, is something like mere musing, a learning activity that requires close observation. "Meditation," on the other hand, "is attentive thought repeated or voluntarily maintained in the mind, to arouse the will to holy and wholesome affections and resolutions."[31] Stevens' poem is a meditation in this authentic sense. Penelope "has composed, so long, a self with which to welcome him," a self composed and shaped through lifelong meditation. Through her meditations she has come in touch with her deepest desires and even experiences glimmers of their fulfillment. When Ulysses comes, Penelope would wait for nothing but his presence; thus, in a poem written just three years before his death, Stevens dwells securely and serenely in the world, the vacancies and emptiness of human existence being not ends in themselves but opening up, through meditation, into a larger reality which is trustworthy and totally fulfilling.

The two halves of the poet's world are thus brought together "in a deep-founded sheltering," as "friend and dear friend." The phrase "friend and dear friend" is repeated with tenderness and warmth as the poem nears its conclusion. It immediately reminds the religious reader of St. Teresa of Avila's famous definition of contemplative prayer:

> Contemplative prayer in my opinion is nothing else than a close sharing between friends; it means taking time frequently to be alone with him who we know loves us.[32]

Stevens' exterior life continued its uneventful course. What was not easily seen was the extreme asceticism of the inner life and its fidelity to the poetic vocation, and the man himself at that venerable age still willing to purge himself of all falsity:

How many poems he denied himself
In his observant progress, lesser things
Than the relentless contact he desired.[33]

For a comprehensive account of the poet's life, many
resources are now available, including Joan Richardson's two-
volume biography, the letters and journals that have been published, the collection which came out in 1977 called *Souvenirs
and Prophesies: The Young Wallace Stevens*, edited by his daughter
Holly, and, to mention only a few, such helpful studies as
George Lensing's *Wallace Stevens: A Poet's Growth*, Milton Bates'
Wallace Stevens: A Mythology of Self and Joseph Riddel's *The
Clairvoyant Eye*. Peter Brazeau's oral biography published in
1983, *Parts of a World: Wallace Stevens Remembered*, properly has
been termed by Dana Gioia one of the few indispensable books
about Stevens. Before Brazeau's work appeared, Gioia comments, "The intensely private man behind the poems seemed a
mystery. Even now he remains a mystery."[34]

Helen Vendler's spirited rebuttal to the Joan Richardson biography of Stevens may serve as a preliminary appraisal of the poet
and his achievement. Vendler regards the Richardson life as
reductionist and excessively psychoanalytical. Admiring justly
Stevens' fidelity to poetry as a higher art, Vendler does not hesi-
tate to describe his life in heroic terms—an unmapped and
frightening voyage to the source.

The extreme heroism of his poetic life—as he abandoned
the received poetic of his century, vowed himself to an
exhausting accuracy of registration and perception, tested
his powers by examining and rejecting work he believed to
be inferior, and persisted through solitude and overwork
toward the creation of new forms of language—would, if it
were the governing concept, produce a very different sort
of biography. The heroism of writing is an unthinkable
venture into the unknown, as unmapped and frightening
as any voyage to the source of the Amazon, as powerful
and daring in its conception as the far gaze of Pascal or the
abyss of Wittgensteinian skepticism. This could be the

premise of a different biography. Its tone would be one of wonder, even amazement, that the wager of genius was won against the odds of provincialism, a lifetime of responsible work, and a trying marriage.[35]

"Everyone enjoys stories of double lives and secret identities," Dana Gioia writes. "Children have Superman; intellectuals have Wallace Stevens."[36]

The twice-mentioned mending of the trees at the arrival of spring confirms in "The World as Meditation" that the universe, though stripped of our projections and illusions, is disclosive of benevolence. In the book of Genesis the same argument is made: the faithfulness of the seasons in their uninterrupted succession reveals an order that can be trusted. "While the earth remains, seedtime and harvest, cold and heat, summer and winter, day and night, shall not cease."[37] It is to how God can be found through the weathers and seasons of the earth we now turn.

NOTES

[1] "Local Objects," in OP, 137.

[2] "Adagia," in OP, 185.

[3] Harold Bloom, *The Western Canon: The Books and School of the Ages* (New York: Harcourt Brace, 1994) 61.

[4] "Farewell to Florida," in CP, 118.

[5] "The Bed of Old John Zeller," in CP, 326.

[6] "The Old Lutheran Bells at Home," in CP, 461.

[7] Milton J. Bates, *Wallace Stevens: A Mythology of Self* (Berkeley: University of California, 1985) 50.

[8] "World without Peculiarity," in CP, 453–54.

[9] Peter Brazeau, *Parts of a World: Wallace Stevens Remembered. An Oral Biography* (New York: Random House, 1983) 150.

[10] Mary McCarthy, *The Groves of Academe* (London: Weidenfeld and Nicolson 1980) 268.

[11] Harriet Monroe, *A Poet's Life,* cited by William Van O'Connor, *The Shaping Spirit: A Study of Wallace Stevens* (Chicago: Henry Regnery, 1950) 11.

[12] "Adagia," in OP, 191.

[13] Interview with the author, Torrington, Conn., April 12, 1993.

[14] Brazeau, *Parts of a World,* 10.

[15] Roland H. Lange, "Poet in Pinstripes," *The Hartford Courant,* Sunday, August 1, 1993, sec. C, 1.

[16] L, 272.

[17] "Of the Surface of Things," in CP, 57.

[18] "Palace of the Babies," in CP, 77.

[19] "Notes toward a Supreme Fiction," in CP, 386.

[20] "An Ordinary Evening in New Haven," in CP, 475.

[21] Florence Berkman, "My Neighbor, the Governor," *Northeast: The Hartford Courant Sunday Magazine,* August 8, 1993, 14–15.

[22] Brazeau, *Parts of a World,* 43.

[23] L, 80.

[24] O'Connor, *The Shaping Spirit,* 4.

[25] "Tea at the Palaz of Hoon," in CP, 65.

[26] See George S. Lensing, *Wallace Stevens: A Poet's Growth* (Baton Rouge: Louisiana State, 1986) 221–22.

[27] Mark Strand, *Hopper* (Ecco), cited by John Updike,

"Hopper's Polluted Silence," *New York Review of Books* 42 (August 10, 1995) 19.

[28] "An Ordinary Evening in New Haven," in CP, 482.

[29] Joseph Carroll, *Wallace Stevens' Supreme Fiction: A New Romanticism* (Baton Rouge: Louisiana State, 1987) 322.

[30] "The World as Meditation," in CP, 521.

[31] Francis de Sales, *A Treatise on the Love of God* (1630), VI, ii, cited by Louis L. Martz, "Wallace Stevens: The World as Meditation," in *Literature and Belief,* ed. M.H. Abrams (New York: Columbia, 1958) 157.

[32] *The Collected Works of St. Teresa of Avila,* trans. K. Kavanaugh, O.C.D., and O. Rodriguez, O.C.D. (Washington D.C.: Institute of Carmelite Studies, 1976) I:67.

[33] "The Comedian as the Letter C," in CP, 34.

[34] Dana Gioia, *Can Poetry Matter? Essays on Poetry and American Culture* (St. Paul: Gray Wolf, 1992) 150.

[35] Helen Vendler, *The Music of What Happens: Poems, Poets, Critics* (Cambridge: Harvard, 1988) 86.

[36] Gioia, *Can Poetry Matter?* 124.

[37] Gn 9:22.

2

Pitiful Lovers of Earth:
Finding the Way to God
through the World

In the "never-ending meditation" which was Wallace Stevens' life, his first poetic thoughts were thoughts of earth. Contact with the natural world was essential to his spiritual vitality from his earliest years as a child growing up in Pennsylvania Dutch country. He knew that landscape well and mentally returned to it again and again. He once wrote that "the trouble with the idea of heaven is that it is merely an idea of the earth."[1] Heaven could not be heaven for him unless it included earth, the local objects which he cherished and wished to keep from perishing by writing poems about them.

"The greatest poverty," Stevens said, "is not to live in a physical world."[2] He firmly believed that "the great poems of heaven and hell have been written and the great poem of earth remains to be written."[3] "The earth, men in their earthly implications, is my subject."[4] He wanted nothing more than to be known as an "amoureux perpétuel"[5] of the world.

That intention never left Stevens, although, as Vendler notes, Stevens retained an instinct for heaven, manifested in his magnificent later poems, even as he maintained an instinct for earth.[6] In a letter to the younger poet José Rodríguez Feo written in 1945, Stevens advised:

There is a precious sentence in Henry James, for whom everyday life was not much more than the mere business of living, but, all the same, he separated himself from it. The sentence is...

> To live *in* the world of creation—to get into it and stay in it—to frequent it and haunt it—to *think* intensely and fruitfully—to woo combinations and inspirations into being by a depth and continuity of attention and meditation—this is the only thing.[7]

During his sojourn in New York City, before his ultimate move to Hartford, Stevens continued to enjoy solitary walks into the countryside, walks that could last an entire day. So many of his poems reflect the perspective of the quiet observer, someone on a beach or in a park noticing things, subtleties of color, changes of season and how these affect us.

Stevens, after he moved to Hartford, continued to make regular visits when he was in New York to St. Patrick's Cathedral. Over the years he became familiar enough with its various chapels and shrines that he could point out things to friends. The church and nature, however, did not come together easily in his spiritual life. The problem was both with the church and nature. The church was not sufficiently for him still "rooted in the Palestinian soil"[8] out of which it originally sprang; and nature, in a world after Darwin, had lost its ability to communicate the sacred. In his student journal at Harvard Stevens had confided, "I wish that groves still were sacred or at least something was. I grow tired of the want of faith—the instinct of faith."[9]

The way out of this spiritual dilemma that was presented to him at Harvard was the Romantic idealism which Ralph Waldo Emerson embraced with his Transcendentalist philosophy. Transcendentalism was supposed to be a form of faith that could survive in the modern world after "supernaturalism" became discredited. Nature could retain its religious significance, according to Emerson, if viewed, devoid of all its ugly particulars, by his cosmic eyeball. Emerson felt he could continue to celebrate holy communion but, tellingly, only without the bread and wine. It's the thought that counts. For Stevens, this was no solution.

Santayana called Emerson "the man on stilts."[10] He was also described as being "as sweet as barbed wire."[11] His influence was already on the wane by the time Stevens reached Harvard. In a poem written late in his career, "Looking Across the Fields and Watching the Birds Fly," Stevens ridicules Emerson whom he dubs "Mr. Homburg," the man of "irritating ideas"—no, "irritating minor ideas." Emerson is imagined as "visiting" home in Concord, not really inhabiting it, a town not at the center but "at the edge of things." There he "thinks away" the grass, the trees, the clouds. But a "new scholar" replacing the older will reflect upon the fantasia of life and realize that it is "too big" for our man-made myths,

> A daily majesty of meditation,
> That comes and goes in silences of its own.[12]

The poem ends with Stevens' characterization of Emerson's project as the misguided attempt to put all nature under a human glass, "a glass aswarm with things going as far as they can."[13]

When Wallace Stevens came, therefore, to write his first volume of poetry under the title *Harmonium,* he was striving to make his way through these notions. In that volume he deliberately takes as his subject the "particulars" of life while Emerson had opined that "nothing is of any value in books excepting the transcendental and extraordinary."[14] Stevens, in contrast, believed "A man cannot search life for unprecedented experiences"; "Poetry is a response to the daily necessity of getting the world right."[15]

"Sunday Morning" is among the poems in *Harmonium* outstanding not only in terms of its familiarity but also in its extended reflection about the contrast between nature and revealed religion. Its most striking passages record moments when the spiritual and the physical interpenetrate completely. As we follow Stevens in his search for God through the natural world we begin with "Sunday Morning." We will then consider two later poems, "Angel Surrounded by Paysans" and "St. Armorer's Church from the Outside," poems in which Stevens attempts to describe what a spirituality more tied to earth, and therefore more believable, might be like.

Sunday Morning

Harmonium, Stevens' first published volume of verse, appeared in 1923 when Stevens was forty-three. "Sunday Morning" was among the poems he completed in 1915, the year in which, it might be said, he found his poetic voice. That poem has been called the greatest American poem of the century and one of the most impressive contemplative poems of any age.[16]

Some have described the extended argument, if that is what "Sunday Morning" actually is, as "tightly knit" and therefore difficult to follow. But Stevens did not write reasoned arguments in his poems. He once said he thought "in pools."[17] This is a better way to experience "Sunday Morning," as a succession of images. As we will see, its stanzas are capable of being rearranged without evident damage to its progression. Stanza V is perhaps the most famous, the one in which the poet claims that "death is the mother of beauty." This is a very evocative description of our ultimate dissolution but it does not hold up very well to rational analysis. Reason, however, is not the poet's method.

This is a particularly secular Sunday morning. The lounging female figure has slept late and is having coffee and an orange as she drowses in a sunny chair. She is not in church on this traditional day of Christian worship. She finds contentment in her surroundings: the opulence of the room, the abundance of nature outside.

Reading "Sunday Morning" aloud brings forth its musical cadences which are so stately, almost like the hush of a formal church service. The pattern of the luxuriant images is reminiscent of an Impressionist painting. One set of images in particular could almost be a Matisse. The oriental rug on the floor with its bird design, the oranges on the table, the vivid greens, the "odalisque" on her chaise in her dressing gown—it could be a scene from Vence where Matisse painted, an earthly paradise. Matisse-like also is the ring of chanting men singing an ecstatic song to the sun, evoking the various versions Matisse painted of female dancers dancing to a music we can only imagine.

Themes that would prove to be constant with Stevens emerge

in "Sunday Morning," the sun, the seasons, the various weathers that mirror our souls:

> Divinity must live within herself:
> Passions of rain, or moods in falling snow;
> Grievings in loneliness, or unsubdued
> Elations when the forest blooms; gusty
> Emotions on wet roads on autumn nights;
> All pleasures and all pains, remembering
> The bough of summer and the winter branch.
> These are the measures destined for her soul.[18]

But two intruders invade this paradisiacal scene and the thoughts of the musing woman: death and religion.

Death, the finality of it, seems to intensify the feeling of how precious is our earthly life. Maybe this is all the paradise we need, so sensuously evoked in the stanzas of the poem through sight, sound and smell. There is more tragic beauty in the ripe fruit falling than in fruit forever frozen in a perfect sky. The tragedy of World War I, which brought human death to a level unknown before in history, provides the background of these brave musings.

The mocking, skeptical side of the poet emerges in his description of the supposed Christian paradise which would have us picking strings of "insipid" lutes. This ironic edge will become less sharp as Stevens matures and settles comfortably into his meditative style in the later poems.

Since this is Sunday, the Christian sabbath commemorating Christ's resurrection from the dead, Palestine enters her thoughts. The tomb in Palestine, once considered a porch for the spirit, is merely a grave, the place where they put Jesus' body. How could it be otherwise in a world without the benevolent design of a creator? Evoking Darwin, the poem describes the earth as an old chaos of the sun, unsponsored and "free."

Still the woman expresses her desire for divinity, something more substantial than the shadowy and dreamlike. "Divinity must live within herself," she concludes, and having come to this realization of a paradise on earth, she finds the sky "friendlier." The "dividing and indifferent blue" of a purely spiritual afterlife holds no sense and is happily discarded.

"Sunday Morning" concludes with the descent of the pigeons. Why pigeons? Stevens is deliberately evoking an ordinary bird, a pest even, instead of the more noble nightingale of poetry or the spiritual dove of religion. The flocks of these pigeons are said to be "casual," just an everyday phenomenon. They do not soar upward but sink downward, downward to darkness "on extended wings."

Helen Vendler makes much of these final, beautiful lines that conclude the poem in the version given in the *Collected Poems.* Stevens, she claims, is here repudiating the Christian notions of heaven and of divinity itself. But the birds' downward flight is described in the poem as "ambiguous." Ambiguity is the more Stevens-like posture. The perceived notions of heaven and divinity may not serve anymore, so the poet may be seeking out something fresher, truer, something more related to our earthly life. We recall in this regard how Jesus himself transposed the soaring eagle as the symbol of divine protection in the Bible into a barnyard hen, thus deliberately joining the sacred with the profane and everyday reality.[19] "In the deceptively mundane resides the holy"; this is the ambiguity addressed in "Sunday Morning."[20]

Stevens was always reticent about assigning intentions and meanings to his poems. Poems evoke more than can be said about them and even exceed their creator. Nonetheless he did make some comments about where he was in his artistic and spiritual life when he wrote the poems gathered into *Harmonium.* "I remarked that when *Harmonium* was in the making," Stevens commented, "there was a time when I liked the idea of images and images alone, or images and the music of verse together. I then believed in *pure poetry* as it was called."[21] Regarding "Sunday Morning" specifically, the poet claimed that it "is not essentially a woman's meditation on religion and the meaning of life....The poem is merely an expression of paganism, although, of course, I did not think that I was expressing paganism when I wrote it."[22]

"Sunday Morning" exists in two printed versions. Harriet Monroe, the editor of *Poetry* magazine in which "Sunday Morning" made its first appearance, dropped two of the eight stanzas that comprise the version in the *Collected Poems* and rearranged the rest so that the seventh stanza appears now as the conclusion. Stanza eight, which in the Monroe version becomes stanza two, resumes the theme of stanza one, the tomb of Jesus in Palestine. Commentators have been puzzled why the poet allowed Monroe so to alter his work. Was Stevens that diffident? A more plausible explanation is that stanza seven is a valid alternative ending; in fact, it bears out the interpretation Stevens later gave to the poem, namely, that in it he was attempting to be "pagan."

"Paganism" I take to mean an attempt to find a more adequate religious appraisal of our earthly life. Christian notions seem to have been rocked by the discoveries of science. Romantic idealism of the Transcendental variety, according to Stevens, is just another human-centered myth projected on the universe. Stevens thus is left to celebrate the physical and immerse himself in its brute reality. The images in *Harmonium* are thus sometimes ugly:

> We hang like warty squashes, streaked and rayed,
> The laughing sky will see the two of us
> Washed into rinds by rotting winter rains.[23]

The pigeons that go downward instead of upward express the fervent desire of the poet that the traditional Christian faith he was brought up in might become more connected to life as we know it and have to live it. After all, the ladder-link between heaven and earth in Jacob's dream in the Bible had angels upon it that went downward to earth as well as upward to heaven.[24]

In any case Stevens could not long be satisfied with wallowing in the mud. Soon there would be angel sightings.

Angel Sightings

As Stevens' comment about the unconscious paganism behind "Sunday Morning" implies, this position, once explored completely, could not be sustained. *Harmonium* proved to be a poetic dead end. A long interval followed before Stevens could regroup himself and strike off in a new direction. As Vendler properly perceives, "...[T]he Stevens of guzzling, rankness, and bluster disappoints and is false."[25] *Harmonium* also contains a mock-epic poem intended to be a modern remake of Dante's *Divine Comedy*, "The Comedian as the Letter C." In it, Stevens makes fun of his hero, the self-deluding Crispin, for his Romantic notions about the world:

> The words of things entangle and confuse.
> The plum survives its poems.[26]

But once you have claimed that a plum, after all, is only a plum, where do you go poetically from there? "Like Crispin," Vendler writes, "Crispin has only two choices in respect to the natural world: to be repelled by it, or to abstract it and make it scan."[27] The question is also where do you go not only poetically but spiritually from there.

It is not infrequent in human affairs that when the sacred is denied or ignored, life becomes flat and one-dimensional. Secularism, it seems, can only go so far before the human spirit rebels against its aridity.[28] It is happening once more as we come to the end of the enlightened twentieth century and angels are making a comeback. Wallace Stevens fervently believed in angels. He even called them "necessary." The angels he believed in were not the kind with long tresses and wings, but angels nonetheless. After discussing his poem, "Angel Surrounded by Paysans," we will look at another of his later poems, "St. Armorer's Church from the Outside," which gives greater detail to the kind of spiritual dimension of life which he was seeking. Both poems draw their inspiration from France, the land of fantasy and intellectual stimulation for Stevens.

In 1949, on the occasion of his seventieth birthday, Stevens imported a still life by the French painter Tal Coat. It featured a Venetian vase with a few terrines, bottles and glasses. Stevens liked it immediately and gave it a name, "Angel Surrounded by Paysans." We can imagine his glancing at it quickly and seeing the vase as an angel, then looking again and finding the angel had disappeared. This approximately is the fantasy from which the poem of that title emerged.

The figure in the poem is described as "half seen, or seen for a moment" like an apparition, and then is quickly, "too quickly," gone. But the angelic visitor is described as "of reality" and, further, as "the necessary angel of earth." Stevens emphatically rejected any interpretation that suggested the angel represented the imagination.[29] This angel, however, is not the winged and haloed variety which is too "tepid" for what he has in mind.

This angel is in fact "one of you" and of the earth, and that is the angel's great value and importance. The necessary function which the angel performs is to allow us to revision the earth and to liberate it from the arid, resistant human-centeredness we have engendered upon it. The earth thus freshly seen yields up watery words whose meaning is not totally clear because it is so subtle.

The poem provides the title of a collection of prose pieces that Stevens put together, *The Necessary Angel.* In his introduction to these essays, Stevens elaborates upon the angel's necessary function which is akin to that of poetry itself. "The real," he writes, "is constantly being engulfed in the unreal." Poetry clears away the unreality by illuminating and enlarging life itself. In doing so it must not resort to any form of mystification for life does not require this kind of human elevation.[30]

The nobility which the angel reveals is actually the spiritual dimension of life which Stevens describes as that which gives life its "height and depth." Like the angel which too quickly disappears and whose words are only partly understood, "nothing," he explains, "could be more evasive and inaccessible, nothing distorts itself and seeks disguises more quickly,"[31] than the spiritual aspect of life. But for all that it is the more precious and "necessary."

We turn now to the poem written in 1952 in which Stevens actually tries to describe what such a spirituality might be like, "St. Armorer's Church from the Outside." According to Stevens this poem was intended to be "Matisse at Vence and a great deal more than that."[32] Matisse got the commission after World War II to ornament a new chapel which became one of the great achievements of his old age. We recall that when Matisse's hands became too arthritic to hold a paint brush, he made the cut-out designs of mass vestments. Stevens admired Matisse the artist but was less comfortable with his traditional Catholicism. Instead of renewing an old form such as Matisse did, the poet decides to construct his own new chapel underneath the fictional church's ancient walls. His perspective upon the church at this point is definitely "from the outside."

The original church building was ruined in the devastation following World War II. The poem was occasioned by a postcard sent from Italy by Barbara Church, the widow of his friend Henry Church. The poet decides to build his own chapel on the same site rather than reconstruct the original. But he accepts the fact that it is on the same site that he is erecting his own chapel because it is part of the same "final seriousness" of the older building but "a new account of everything old."

The chapel like the more grand edifice that is now "sacked" above it, fulfills the same spiritual need: "a sign of meaning in the meaningless," "a civilization formed from the outward blank."

The new representation of the sacred is needed because the sacred itself is "always beginning...over and over," and can never be adequately represented. Each generation must give a new account of it, give it the life, the "dizzle-dazzle" which it deserves.

The new chapel will be the renewed "yes" spoken upon life, the acceptance of the prose of life, ordinary things like fruit that's for sale in the market every day. It will be a "yes" spoken by the present generation that must be itself and live fully in the natural world.

The older church was noble, but now it is in ruins; a tree grows where the altar once was. But this is not a disaster, because the tree itself is a sign of life that is always renewing itself. The new chapel, though modest, is also closer to the earth, more related to the earth, more connected and "natural."

Finding God on Earth

The poet's first reaction as recorded in "Sunday Morning" was that divinity must be unreal because the world doesn't need it anymore to explain its origins and because it is something shadowy and dreamlike in any case. He progresses to the point of realizing that the desire for divinity, such as the musing woman manifested in "Sunday Morning," is not merely nostalgia but "necessary" if we are to get the world right. The world manifests a nobility and grandeur which we can see only from another, nonhuman perspective. Divinity is so evanescent, not because it is unreal, but because it is so subtle a reality: it takes the reach of poetry to discern its fleeting appearance that is so easily missed and misunderstood.

If, then, there is a "supernatural"—and there is—such a reality must be seen in its intimate relation to all that is natural. Christianity, on the other hand, has tended to separate the supernatural into a separate zone to protect it but, in the process, has found itself without credibility. Religious people cannot be asked to live their lives in separate compartments, the natural and the supernatural, the everyday and the religious. They must be helped to see the true nobility of their lives.

The advocates of traditional religious institutions are forever trying to explain the supernatural as if everyone already knows about the natural. In fact, it is the natural that needs explaining, the earthly that needs a new account. Too often we cannot know what is natural, what is real, because we distort it with our own limited horizon.

Stevens thus made substantial progress in his spiritual search. He reached the point in "St. Armorer's Church" that he could render an account of the sacred that he knew and still be himself: "And there he walks and does as he lives and likes."

But he was still to deal with a lurking and underlying personal uncomfortableness: his tendency to prefer the offbeat and the half-tones of life. How he came to accept this as something positive in himself rather than a negative and how he worked through it to a deeper realization of God is the subject to which we now turn.

The chapel he ultimately builds for God to dwell in is close to the earth. It is in this sense like Jacob's resting upon the ground and discovering the place inhabited by angels. But as in Jacob's story, the place upon the ground is not just any place: God's dwelling on earth must be the portion of it which we cherish and love, that we feel connected with, something close to home. This is exactly how Stevens expresses it in his most moving tribute to a fellow poet, John Crowe Ransom, written late in life, but a tribute which speaks volumes about what Stevens himself was aiming for. Poetry, he wrote, is

> a vital affair, not an affair of the heart (as it may in one's first poems), but an affair of the whole being (as in one's last poems), a fundamental affair of life, or, rather, an affair of fundamental life; so that one's cry O Jerusalem becomes little by little a cry to something a little nearer and nearer until at last one cries out to a living name, a living place, a living thing, and in crying out confesses openly to all the bitter secretions of experience.[33]

Besides dwelling upon earth, the mysterious divine presence also resides within the heights and depths of the human person. It is to the interior conversion between the human person and the object of our fondest desires that we now turn.

NOTES

1 L, 464.

2 "Esthétique du Mal," in CP, 325.

3 "Imagination as Value" (essay), in NA, 142.

4 "The Irrational Element in Poetry" (essay), in OP, 232–33.

5 "The Noble Rider and the Sound of Words" (essay), in NA, 30.

6 Helen Vendler, *On Extended Wings: Wallace Stevens's Longer Poems* (Cambridge: Harvard, 1969) 45.

7 Cited by Samuel French Morse, *Wallace Stevens: Poetry as Life* (New York: Pegasus, 1970) 197.

8 L, 140.

9 Cited by Nathan A. Scott, Jr., *The Poetics of Belief: Studies in Coleridge, Arnold, Pater, Santayana, Stevens and Heidegger* (Chapel Hill: University of North Carolina, 1985) 142.

10 George Santayana, *The Last Puritan: A Memoir in the Form of a Novel* (New York: Charles Scribner's Sons, 1949) 186.

11 Cited by Harold Bloom, *The American Religion* (New York: Simon and Schuster, 1992) 182.

12 "Looking Across the Fields and Watching the Birds Fly," in CP, 518.

13 Ibid., 519.

14 Ralph Waldo Emerson, *The Portable Emerson,* ed. Carl Bode with Malcolm Cowley (New York: Penguin, 1981) 258.

15 "Adagia," in OP, 197, 201.

16 Yvor Winters, *In Defense of Reason* (New York: Swallow and Morrow, 1947) 476.

17 "Adagia," in OP, 196.

18 "Sunday Morning," in CP, 67.

19 "How often have I longed to gather your children as a hen gathers her chicks under her wings and you refused!" (Mt 23:37).

20 Dean Wentword Bethea, "Sunday Morning at the Clavier: A Comparative Approach to Teaching Stevens," in *Teaching Wallace Stevens: Practical Essays* ed. John N. Serio and B.J. Leggett (Knoxville: University of Tennessee, 1994) 224.

21 L, 288.

22 L, 250.

23 "Le Monocle de Mon Oncle," in CP, 16.

[24] Gn 28:12.

[25] Vendler, *On Extended Wings,* 54.

[26] "The Comedian as the Letter C," in CP, 41.

[27] Vendler, *On Extended Wings,* 49.

[28] David Blackbourn in his book, *Marpingen: Apparitions of the Virgin Mary in Nineteenth Century Germany* (New York: Alfred A. Knopf, 1994) recasts our interpretation of the nineteenth century which not only saw the rise of the secular modern state and the crisis of modernity but also gave rise to a religious reaction and revival of popular piety.

[29] George S. Lensing, *Wallace Stevens: A Poet's Growth* (Baton Rouge: Louisiana State, 1986) 280.

[30] Introduction, NA, viii.

[31] "The Noble Rider and the Sound of Words" (essay), in NA, 34.

[32] Lensing, *A Poet's Growth,* 100.

[33] "John Crowe Ransom: Tennessean" (essay), in OP, 248.

3

The Interior Paramour: Finding God within Oneself

"God is in me or is not at all (does not exist),"[1] Wallace Stevens once jotted down in one of his "asides." In this chapter we will follow Stevens in his ruthless self-questioning and self-examination, a search which took him beyond his innermost self to the frontiers of the knowledge of God.

Stevens in his early poetry was a man of many masks, all of them displaying his lively wit and many of them bordering on the outrageous and grandiose. He cast himself among other roles as the noble hidalgo, the knight in the service of a great cause. In all of these masks he became the self-described "Professor Eucalyptus" (literally, "well-hidden") who tried on these various disguises because he really was not sure who he was or how he fitted into the world. His true feelings had to be covered over with intellectual observations because they were too confusing or powerful to handle.

Seven years were to elapse after the publication of *Harmonium,* his first collection of poems that received such a poor public reception before his second collection, *Ideas of Order,* made its appearance. He had other things to distract him at the time—advancement in the insurance company, the birth of his daughter, the disintegration of his marriage. But underneath, things were stirring. *Harmonium,* in its celebration of his physical side, took him only so far and proved to be an artistic and spiritual dead end. It was a time for him to say his farewells to Florida, that "venereal soil" of warmth and fertility, and set his course in the direction of his native climate, the colder North, the land of his religious forebears and place of introspection.

So many commentators have missed this shaping religious center in Stevens. They either play up his celebration of the satisfactions of earthly existence as manifested in the early poems, or emphasize the dissatisfactions with prevailing religious conceptions that are the recurrent theme of the later poetry, taking them to express a fundamental disbelief. In both cases Stevens is mistaken for a man who dwelt more in his head than in his heart.

The early appraisal by Louis Untermeyer is typical. In his anthology, *Modern American Poetry,* which went through several editions in the 1920s, Untermeyer understands Stevens to be "a poet of peculiar reticences." Nonetheless he compares Stevens' poems to Impressionist paintings, lamenting that in them "emotion itself seems to be absent" and that they are "beyond thought of any kind." They are "little related to any human struggle," he goes on. "Such poems," Untermeyer concludes, in dismissing them except for their technical brilliance, "have much for the eye, something for the ear but little indeed for the central hunger which is at the heart of all the senses."[2]

The poet was noted for his "reticences." Even in the poems in which he poured out so much of himself, the reflections are given in the third-person at some remove from the personal emotion which prompted them. His stated theme for all his poetry was the interplay, the mutual dependence, between reality and imagination, but even here the interest for this most philosophical of poets was not merely philosophical. We have to ask why this man who wanted so much to be a physical being at home in the world was so obviously uncomfortable in his attempts to be such? Why was there such a great gulf between his reality and his imagination?

The answer to these questions is at the heart of Stevens' spiritual search. Stevens, for all his attempts to use the mind to divert from emotion, was a person of passionate feeling. Far from feeling too little, Stevens felt too much. Helen Vendler, who has studied Stevens for a long time and greatly admires him, describes him accurately as a man who knew catastrophic disappointment, bitter solitude and personal sadness.[3] Often he confesses an absence of feelings, she explains, a blank, but that is because he feels too much. "He has been read too little," she states, "as a poet of human misery."[4]

But what was this "misery"? It was more than misery in the usual sense. It had to do with the void, the absence that Stevens found in the center of his existence.[5] It had to do with what he called the "poverty" of the world we inhabit, its radical insufficiency to satisfy our deepest cravings and desires and its destiny to ultimate dissolution.

Stevens' father always thought him a man who might not fare well in this world, a dreamer. His business associates found him arrogant and peculiar. The companions he sought out through membership in Hartford's Canoe Club also found him odd and thought of expelling him. His marriage was, though he refused to talk about it, a failure; his only child, a disappointment. But, spiritually speaking, Stevens' most significant "misery" was within himself.

One of the ways this personal misery manifested itself was in what some have termed his "over-anxiousness" on the subject of religion. More accurately described, Wallace Stevens' misery was of a spiritual nature that ultimately opened him up to the abysses and forces that showed the inadequacy of all his previous conceptions of who he was. Painfully encountering them and not backing away will prove to be for Stevens the route not only to his self-discovery—becoming himself and accepting himself at least without the masks—but also to his encounter with God.

In this chapter we will first see an example of Stevens' self-questioning to the point of self-loathing, the poem "The Motive for Metaphor." We will then follow him in his attempts to name the Nameless One in those masterful poems he collected under the title, "Notes Toward a Supreme Fiction." We will also accompany him in his ultimate and fulfilling encounter with the God he discovered within himself as recorded in the poem, "Final Soliloquy to the Interior Paramour." We will then offer some concluding comments relating the spiritual quest of Wallace Stevens to that of St. Ignatius of Loyola.

"The Motive for Metaphor"

Milton J. Bates, in his illuminating study of Stevens' poetry, *The Mythology of Self,* takes as his motif Stevens' various attempts to reinvent himself. For various reasons Stevens found himself to be always the outsider. The poems reveal the posture of one who, not daring to be the protagonist, is the perennial observer. Not comfortable to speak in his own name and voice, he assumes the roles of various characters that are often outlandish. He cringes from human intimacy, admitting his life is more a series of places than of persons. His ultimate goal was to become "a person in charge of himself."[6]

Included within the same volume of poems as "Notes Toward a Supreme Fiction" is the poem of severe and harsh self-accusation, "The Motive for Metaphor." In it the poet reveals himself to an uncharacteristic degree as in a condition of full spiritual transition. The dust jacket of this volume of poems published under the title *Transport to Summer* records in the 1951 edition that when Wallace Stevens received the Bollingen Prize in Poetry from Yale University Library, "it was widely stated that he had been honored as a poet whose unwavering growth over a long period of time was continuing." The prize was awarded in 1949, and for such a remark to have been able to be made only six years before the poet's death gives some indication of the quality and depth of Wallace Stevens' lifelong spiritual journey.

"The Motive for Metaphor" expresses the poet's extreme dissatisfaction with himself. He calls everything into question, including the worth and value of everything he ever wrote. The motive for all his poems he now realizes was evasion: he was shrinking from himself and from the world as it really is. That is why he has been living in his imagination and for so long has been avoiding daylight reality.

> The obscure moon lighting an obscure world
> Of things that would never be quite expressed,
> Where you yourself were never quite yourself
> And did not want nor have to be.[7]

Looking at himself with searing honesty, "you," he says, accusatorially, prefer things "half dead" as in autumn, your favorite season, when the wind moves "like a cripple." Spring once appealed to you for the same reason, a season "[w]ith the half colors of quarter-things." Everything you have written until now is mere repetition of the same tired themes, and therefore "words without meaning."

Even worse, he confesses, the very things he expressed desire for continue to elude him. His futile exhilarations and discovered order in life simply cannot withstand rational examination.

When a person is in such a state, all mistaken complacency, which is fatal to the spiritual life, is set aside, and the stage is set for new spiritual growth.

As Stevens confronts the limited and limiting "motive" behind all his poetry until then, namely, shirking from reality and retreating into imagination, a new horizon was being disclosed, the level of existence where his deepest longings and desires resided. From this center of his authentic self a new poetry can now emerge.

> But the priest desires. The philosopher desires.
>
> And not to have is the beginning of desire...
>
> From this the poem springs: that we live in a place
> That is not our own and, much more, not ourselves
> And hard it is in spite of blazoned days.[8]

Naming the Nameless One

William James, the esteemed philosopher of religion, was still teaching at Harvard when Stevens was a student there. It was James who used the phrase "will to believe" as a basic instinct of the human heart. This "will," which has nothing to do with "willpower" as such but refers to a fundamental orientation of our lives, perdures, according to James, even when the human heart has no credible object to believe in. Now that previous conceptions of divinity have been called into question by the scientific worldview, James offered in their place a brilliant account of religious conversion and mystical experience in his classic work, *The Varieties of Religious Experience*.[9] Stevens in "Notes toward a Supreme Fiction" uses the term "notes" to describe these poems because of their probing and tentative nature, but in them he accepts James' general position but goes beyond it. Stevens attempts to name the object of our will to believe. In daring to do this Stevens utilizes what he calls "fictions."

The Latin root of the English word "fiction" is *fingere*, which has two meanings that are quite distinct, one being positive, the other, decidedly negative. A fiction can be a calculated invention to reveal something true that could not otherwise be expressed, or it can refer to an unreal imagining as in a figment of the imagination or in a mental error.[10] With Stevens the term is used in the positive sense of a calculated risk. A fiction, according to Stevens, is a "living changingness"[11] that points beyond itself to a reality which human reason finds impossible to pin down. The parables of Jesus are truthful fictions in this same way because the parables attempt to give earthly equivalents of the heavenly kingdom. Nicholas of Cusa, a theologian of the late Middle Ages (1401–1446), similarly employed what he called "symbols" whose oscillation between themselves and what is being evoked stimulate our imaginations to grasp a reality beyond our understanding or power to explain. In a way similar to Jesus and Nicholas, with Stevens, when we wish greater clarity and more logical argument, we are forever stranded in the realm of the "as if."[12] To make this "fictional" approach to the Nameless One work, you have to assume the stance of what Cusa called "learned ignorance." To know God truly you have to unlearn everything you thought you knew about God. All we humans can know about God is *that* God is and very little of *what* God is. With regard to ultimate reality, all we have are

illustrations, parallel thoughts, metaphors, symbols, "fictions" if
you will—the "as if."

Thus Stevens in the "Notes" writes:

> You must become an ignorant man again
> And see the sun again with an ignorant eye
> And see it clearly in the idea of it.[13]

The foundation of this approach may be found in the words of
St. Paul: "We see now through a mirror in enigma; but then we
shall be seeing face to face."[14] Following Paul, Cusa would state,
"In theological matters, negations are true and affirmations
inadequate."[15] Stevens on his part maintains that the Supreme
Fiction is itself poetry, a metaphor: something whose form is
elusively perceived even as we question its validity. Stevens
once said that "adoration is a form of face to face. We struggle
with the face and sense it everywhere and try to express the
changes."[16]

With this as a background we are in a better position to
understand what Wallace Stevens is attempting in "Notes
toward a Supreme Fiction." "Poetry is the supreme fiction,"
Stevens explained in a letter, the poetry that is "trying to create
something as valid as the idea of God has been."[17] God, of
course, is more than "idea," as Stevens himself would say.

The life setting of "Notes toward a Supreme Fiction" may be
found in the circumstances the poet found himself in during
1942. Close family members had died and World War II was rag-
ing, bringing human destruction of enormous scale. The spiritual role of the poet which Stevens fervently upheld required
that he stake out the position of poetry in the face of the human
condition and its tragic transitoriness. Helen Vendler regards
"Notes" as a study of "deity in decline." They are better read as a
poetic testimony to the ever new spiritual dimension of the
world.

Stevens attributes three qualities to the Supreme Fiction: it
must be abstract; it must change; it must give pleasure.

It Must Be Abstract

"Abstraction" refers to the process of getting beyond surface reality to the spiritual essence beneath. "Abstract" painters, for example, feel the spiritual need not so much to describe the exteriors of things as to probe their own feelings toward them, especially feelings of alienation. Stevens writes in "Notes":

> It is the celestial ennui of apartments
> That sends us back to the first idea.[18]

"Apartments" connote "a-partments," that is to say, our spiritual condition in the modern world of being out of joint.

Robert Motherwell, the abstract expressionist painter, felt that Stevens, more than any other modern poet, expressed what he himself was trying to achieve artistically. Motherwell explains what "abstraction" means to him:

> Abstract art is a true mysticism—I dislike the word—or rather a series of mysticisms that grew up in the historical circumstances that all mysticisms do, from a primary sense of gulf, an abyss, a void between one's lonely self and the world. Abstract art is an effort to close the void that modern men feel. Its abstraction is its emphasis.[19]

When Stevens, therefore, in "Notes" says, "It must be abstract," he means, not that we are leaving the particulars of life to arrive at a more elevated plane, but rather that we faithfully remain with life's particulars to see them for the first time, in their full reality. "Abstraction," however, is not easily achieved. Our human-centered conceptions always get in the way. We tend to see everything from our limited point of view. In doing so, we often falsify and romanticize things, imposing upon them our idealizations and emotions. Furthermore, we are held back because, given our scientific worldview, we tend to be skeptical of anything that human reason cannot measure.

Through poetry's abstraction we become present at the Creation, when things were freshest. We begin to believe in "an immaculate beginning" that will result in "an immaculate end."

From this newfound candor of perception we experience a unique exhilaration.[20]

The bright sun of reality, being "inconceivable," can have no name, an admonition repeated over and over again in this section:

> How clean the sun when seen in its idea,
> Washed in the remotest cleanliness of a heaven
> That has expelled us and our images...
>
> There is a project for the sun. The sun
> Must bear no name, gold flourisher, but be
> In the difficulty of what it is to be.[21]

What Stevens is practicing here is what Christian tradition calls the "negative way," the way of denying the adequacy of any human conception of God. "It must be abstract" as a divine attribute may make the Supreme Fiction appear to be unreal or even agnostic. In fact it is an approach to something eternally fresh and forever new.

It Must Change

The Supreme Fiction also "must change," be in fact "living changedness," because it is alive and ever being born. "Living changedness" is not too distant an equivalent of the definition of God in the book of Exodus: "I am who I am," God responds from the burning bush when Moses asks his name.[22] That biblical definition is both an evasion and a hint: God's name cannot be known, but God will be known in what God does, how he subtly manifests himself through what he does.

The preaching by the leaders of the church sadly, for Stevens, falls far short of presenting this ever-changing freshness of God. In a famous and funny poem in this section, the poem of the birds, the unchanging chirping of these "tireless chorister[s]," repeating "[a] single text, with granite monotony," is compared with the preachings of bloodless bishops, "minstrels lacking minstrelsy."[23]

The bird chirp of the sparrow, rendered "bethou me," is how the poet hears these deadly sermons:

> ...Bethou him, you
> And you, bethou him and bethou. It is
> A sound like any other. It will end.[24]

It is up to the poet to supply for the inadequacy of these ecclesiastical birds.

Throughout his life, Stevens did try to keep contact with the church. His problems were less with the church as an organization, which he esteemed, than with the idea of God he inherited. But Stevens could be merciless toward the representatives of the Church, as in this "sermon of the birds."

It Must Give Pleasure

Although Stevens admitted that the Supreme Fiction's attributes are not confined to those he enumerates, he gives only one other, "It must give pleasure." Pleasure here is important, for it includes within itself not only our pleasure in earthly things but also the ultimate fulfillment of all human desire, the ultimate peace and long-sought at-homeness within our physical being. It is important for the poet to be very concrete about life's pleasures and not to divorce them from spiritual fulfillment. He even notes a specific wine (Meursault), the main course (lobster Bombay), the relish (mango chutney).[25]

Until now the critics could be right in their claim that the Supreme Fiction is all about words and nothing but words, the fantastic embellishments of the poet upon a theme. But because the Supreme Fiction "must give pleasure," it must be about more than intellectual exercises and clever imagery—it must have to do with our deepest desires and their fulfillment.

What the poet here is attempting by his fictions is to reach a nothingness, a nakedness, "a point beyond which thought could not progress as thought,"[26] and arrive where reason is of no help and gives way to "irrational distortion." Such fictions arise from need, personal need, from feeling:

> That's it: the more than rational distortion,
> The fiction that results from feeling.[27]

With total self disclosure the poet now expresses the depths of his faith.

> ....But to impose is not
> To discover. To discover an order as of
> A season, to discover summer and know it,
>
> To discover winter and know it well, to find,
> Not to impose, not to have reasoned at all,
> Out of nothing to have come on major weather,
>
> It is possible, possible, possible. It must
> Be possible. It must be that in time
> The real will from its crude compoundings come,
>
> Seeming, at first, a beast disgorged, unlike,
> Warmed by a desperate milk. To find the real,
> To be stripped of every fiction except one,
>
> The fiction of an absolute—Angel...[28]

In this final collection of poems in which God is finally achieved, the poet asks in astonishment, "What am I to believe?" The experience of the self and the experience of God have become almost indistinguishable.

> Is it I then that keep saying there is an hour
> Filled with expressible bliss, in which I have
>
> No need, am happy, forget need's golden hand
> Am satisfied without solacing majesty,
> And if there is an hour there is a day,

> There is a month, a year, there is a time
> In which majesty is a mirror of the self:
> I have not but I am and as I am, I am.[29]

Without expecting it, the poet has come upon "major weather," something frightening and powerful, "like a beast disgorged," but at the same time totally fulfilling, no alien presence but the God within himself.

Final Soliloquy of the Interior Paramour

In a very late poem of exquisite beauty and enormous emotive power, Stevens evoked that state of ultimate blessedness where simply being there "is enough." The old dualisms of reality and imagination have been transcended at last. In his "Final Soliloquy of the Interior Paramour," the evening dark descends upon his life. Here, as elsewhere in his poetry, the evening is a source of maternal comfort and assurance, without any hint of "the terrors of the night." The mood of the poem is of profound repose. There is no nostalgia for the events of the day that is passing, no regrets about projects left undone, mistakes that have been made.

That old fixation, "reason," the mind which can never be satisfied, never, according to Stevens, now appears to be "small." All the old intellectual reservations have been set aside as human obsessions with the literal surface of things. The darkness has served to obscure their effects, so in darkness strangely we can see better what needs to be seen. There is also no hint of bitterness about life's disappointments: the poet is meeting at last his paramour in this most intense rendezvous.

The poet has been liberated at last from the confines of his own introspection: this meeting is not of his making but has been "arranged" for him. He is in a place of warmth, light, power and miracle. The center he has been seeking is achieved. When asked by his correspondent, Sister Bernetta Quinn, whether he believed in God, Stevens truthfully replied, "I do seek a center and expect to go on seeking it."[30]

In this blessed state of self-forgetfulness, God is made manifest as the highest candle our imagination can conceive. Since it is our concept that we project, and not God who is forever beyond conceptualization, it is still merely a candle, but that one candle is a sufficient hint of the center he was seeking. It is light at the end, more light, only light. The spirit without a foyer in this world can now find a dwelling in which to live.

Wallace Stevens and St. Ignatius of Loyola: Hidalgos of God

We have seen in the first chapter how Stevens in his meditations used the imagination as his vehicle in a way similar to the one prescribed in the *Spiritual Exercises* of St. Ignatius of Loyola. The spiritual evolution of Wallace Stevens finds in the life of this great Spanish mystic and Jesuit founder some illuminating parallels and contrasts.

Ignatius (1491–1556) and Stevens lived in very different worlds religiously speaking; Stevens was always pointing out the difference between an age where God's hand is perceived to be everywhere and one where it is detected nowhere. But the dynamics of religious conversion and how it actually occurs can be seen more clearly if we trace the way both men shed previous identities after shattering personal experiences and reemerged with new personal integration.

The process of religious conversion is usually described not so much as the product as of human self-transformation but as an action of divine grace. In the age of Ignatius, such an evolution would be attributed to an "intervention" of God. With his more nuanced appreciation of how grace manifests itself and rejecting all "interventionism" by outside forces, Stevens would offer another explanation. For him, and for us in the modern age, grace, the giftedness of the event and process of conversion, is manifested in the fact that a potentially self-destructive dissolution of previous identity did not actually result in self-destruction but a new integration of spiritual and artistic force.

Ignatius, following in his father's footsteps, up to the age of twenty-six, pursued the career of a dashing hidalgo and courtier. Living within this romantic, adolescent fantasy, Ignatius prized female admiration and sought it through military ventures that were often highly risky. Like Stevens, Ignatius was fastidious about his personal appearance and lived in a world of narcissistic dreams.[31] A cannonball that shattered his leg during the siege of Pamplona put an end to his image of personal invulnerability. It was at this point that there slowly emerged from the crippled Inigo the Hidalgo—Ignatius the religious mystic.

Dependent and helpless during his lengthy recuperation, Ignatius had the leisure to read lives of Christ and of the saints. It was not as if he had not been a believer, but now a new personal ideal began to take shape: instead of serving the king, he would give his services to the King of kings; in place of pursuing his father's career, he would seek the will and favor of the heavenly Father. But none of this became absolutely clear until at Manresa Ignatius underwent frightening episodes that almost led to personal disintegration. It was in a cave at Manresa that he had the vision of the many-eyed serpent, of which he gave the following description:

> It often happened to him in broad daylight to see something in the air close to him, which gave him great consolation because it was very beautiful. He could not make out very clearly what the thing was, but somehow it appeared to have the form of a serpent. It was bright with objects that shone like eyes, although they were not eyes. He found great delight and consolation in looking at this thing, and the more he saw it the greater grew his consolation. When it disappeared, it left him displeased.[32]

Wallace Stevens passed through something like Ignatius' Pamplona experience on the road to his own spiritual conversion. "The Motive for Metaphor," as we have seen, alludes to the poet's shattered self-confidence and refers to his affinity to the "crippled side of things." Stevens also had his own encounter with the frightening serpent which he described in "The Auroras of Autumn," a poem which revealed him plumbing the depths of his own unconscious. It was these personal crises and relentless self-scrutiny that allowed both men to achieve their full spiritual selves. Seeking the center is characteristic of the religious person. This process bravely pursued to the end can result in a new personal integration as well as greatly heightened creative energy. The ultimate form the personalities of both men assumed involved a new identification with the religious piety of their youth but in radically personalized ways that made it their own.

The tendency to grandiose conceptions of one's self has often been perceived in the religious personality; this characteristic also manifested itself in both Ignatius and Stevens. Ignatius considered himself as God's favored one in a way similar to Christ. Stevens likewise for a time was preoccupied with the figure of the "major man," the person of superior perception. In "Notes toward a Supreme Fiction" Stevens comes dangerously close to identifying God the creator with himself. There were times, too, when the poet seems just too full of himself and taken with his own wit.

Ignatius and Stevens in their own ways started off as romantic hidalgos in pursuit of noble dreams. That early romanticism had to be cast off if they were to progress in the spiritual life. In Stevens' case, his shelving the "old" romanticism and seeking a new one has usually been described as his rejection of previous literary influences, but it was much more than this. The stakes were much more personal and serious.

Although the lives of both men display similar illuminating characteristics of what happens to a person who undergoes profound spiritual transformation, the example of Stevens' conversion has strikingly different emphases from that of Ignatius. It is these emphases which place Stevens in certain respects closer to us as a helpful spiritual mentor.

Ignatius' spirituality involved an all-out attack upon the pleasure principle. "To act against nature" (*agere contra*) was his method, and he practiced it by harsh and prolonged penances and fasts that ultimately did damage to his physical health. Stevens, on the other hand, never wavered in his love of earthly pleasures—the wine, the food, the physical beauty. Indifference to worldly delights was not a goal Stevens set for himself as a spiritual ideal, even after all his personal disappointments. Stevens' asceticism was more related to his soul than to his body.

Ignatius in his understanding of God related well to God the Father as the generating Being within the blessed Trinity. Stevens' relationship to God was more in line with John of the Cross: God was often described in nuptial imagery of mutuality and dependence and in maternal ways. In this sense Stevens' spirituality was more Franciscan than Jesuit as he indicated in his mock epic, "The Comedian as the Letter C." The "comedian" who is the protagonist of the poem was partly modeled upon St. Francis of Assisi who with clown-like appearance added bells to his garments to frighten off any creatures that he might have inadvertently stepped upon. We can recall also that Stevens in another place attributed the fundamental error of the modern world to that Jesuit product, René Descartes, whose reliance upon clear and distinct ideas as the criterion of truth has misled, according to Stevens, students at the Sorbonne to this very day.[33]

A mysterious dedication launches "Notes toward a Supreme Fiction." It is not unusual for the artist to invoke the Muse at the start of a major work, but the figure so fervently described as the one uniquely loved seems too close to the person of the poet to be a mere literary convention. The language is extreme unless the being addressed is of the utmost personal significance, the very transparence which reveals the self to the self. Stevens has not yet arrived at the bliss of the "Final Soliloquy of the Interior Paramour," but he is on the way there, on the way to peace within himself:

> And for what, except for you, do I feel love?
> Do I press the extremest book of the wisest man
> Close to me, hidden in me day and night?
> In the uncertain light of single, certain truth,
> Equal in living changingness to the light
> In which I meet you, in which we sit at rest,
> For a moment in the central of our being,
> The vivid transparence that you bring is peace.[34]

Stevens would not be satisfied until he discovered that majesty which is "the mirror of the self."[35] Having rejected an exterior "solacing majesty" which solaces because it *is* exterior, he seeks the majesty which is within. Could it be he in whose image the divine majesty is made, thus reversing Genesis? Stevens is willing to cross these mystical frontiers in search of "the God who must be found in me, or not at all."[36]

NOTES

[1] "Adagia," in OP, 198.

[2] Louis Untermeyer, *Modern American Poetry* (New York: Harcourt, Brace, 1925) 326–27.

[3] Helen Vendler, *Wallace Stevens: Words Chosen Out of Desire* (Knoxville: University of Tennessee, 1984) 11.

[4] Ibid.

[5] "The Man with the Blue Guitar," in CP, 176.

[6] Milton J. Bates, *Wallace Stevens: A Mythology of Self* (Berkeley: University of California, 1985) 31.

[7] "The Motive for Metaphor," in CP, 288.

[8] "Notes toward a Supreme Fiction," in CP, 382–83.

[9] William James, *The Varieties of Religious Experience* (New York: Longmans, Green, first published 1902).

[10] See Ronald Levao, *Renaissance Minds and Their Fictions* (Berkeley: University of California, 1985) 70.

[11] "Notes toward a Supreme Fiction," in CP, 38.

[12] "Notes toward a Supreme Fiction" may profitably be read in the context of the poet's essay, "The Noble Rider and the Sound of Words," in NA, 3–36.

[13] "Notes toward a Supreme Fiction," in CP, 380.

[14] 1 Cor 13:12.

[15] *Docta ignorantia,* 1:26.

[16] L, 438.

[17] L, 435.

[18] "Notes toward a Supreme Fiction," in CP, 381.

[19] *The Collected Writings of Robert Motherwell,* ed. Stephanie Terenzio (New York: Oxford, 1992) 92.

[20] "Notes toward a Supreme Fiction," in CP, 382.

[21] Ibid., 381.

[22] Ex 3:13.

[23] "Notes toward a Supreme Fiction," in CP, 394.

[24] Ibid., 394.

[25] Ibid., 401.

[26] Ibid., 403.

[27] Ibid., 406.

[28] Ibid., 404.

[29] Ibid., 404–5.

[30] L, 584.

³¹ Here I follow the insightful study by the Jesuit psychiatrist W.W. Meisner, S.J., M.D., *Ignatius of Loyola: The Psychology of a Saint* (New Haven: Yale, 1992).

³² Ibid., 71.

³³ "Notes toward a Supreme Fiction," in CP, 406.

³⁴ Ibid., 380.

³⁵ Ibid., 405.

³⁶ In an important article, "The Experience of the Self and the Experience of God," Karl Rahner, S.J., explains how these two experiences are related and how significant they are for a contemporary person's ability to grasp the meaning of God:

> For in this way, it might be possible for modern man, for whom all explicit statements about God fall all too easily under ideological distrust, to have it brought home to him that whether he wants it or not, in the changing history of his relationship with himself...that he has all along been living through a history of his experience of God. (Karl Rahner, S.J., *Theological Investigations,* vol 13 [New York: Crossroad, 1975] 132.)

4

Our Spiritual Climate: A New Ice Age

To his correspondent Hi Simons, Wallace Stevens once explained the significance of weather for him and his poetry: "We are physical beings in a physical world; the weather is one of the things that we enjoy."[1]

Here Stevens is underscoring a basic and stubbornly held conviction of his, namely, "we are physical beings in a physical world"—but he is being typically off-handed and casual about the huge spiritual significance the weather represents for him. To know that, you have to immerse yourself in his poetry and the inner world the weather reveals in it. Stevens above all wished to anchor his spiritual life in reality, in the physical world. Weather for him is "an event," something actual connecting time and space.[2] "The real is only the base," he observed, "but it is the base."[3] For Stevens "the gods come out of the weather," the weather he called "major."[4] Harold Bloom puts it succinctly: Wallace Stevens "seeks his spirit in things of the weather."[5]

In the last chapter we gave attention to the section of "Notes toward a Supreme Fiction" in which Stevens fervently prays that it might be possible by deeply knowing summer, by deeply knowing winter, that he might discover an order, an Angel revealed in the real.[6] Joan Richardson writes that when she is teaching students to read Stevens she explains that the poems require the practice of "sharpened attention," of the kind sailors who go out into the deep need to have if they are to survive whatever lies in

71

wait for them out there. "Out of this practice" of sharpened attention, she continues, "we grasp what prayer used to do or could
do."[7] Stevens put it this way: "Weather is a sense of nature. Poetry
is a sense."[8] Rather than a play of fancy, "Poetry is a response to
the daily necessity of getting the world right."[9]

In this regard I recall a seminarian at the time that I was rector
always sitting, summer or winter, on the same bench every day
to meditate. I once asked him why he did this. He replied that by
having this fixed place in the universe he could detect the subtle
changes that occur as one season passes into the next. In a similar way Wallace Stevens spent hours in Elizabeth Park near his
home sitting and observing the divinity that disguises itself in
subtleties of the weather.

The climatic condition of our spiritual life that Stevens, the
self-described "pundit of the weather,"[10] perceives is decidedly
cold and wintry. It is a kind of new Ice Age that we are passing
through where God is absent like the sun and everything is cold
and bare.

Stevens then begins his spiritual quest by saying his "Farewell
to Florida," one of the first poems after *Harmonium.* He sets sail
for the North, "my North." The ship carries him into the cold, to
a land lying "in a wintry slime."[11] It is a journey North by way of
going inward, focusing now not upon the physical allure of the
tropics but upon the emptiness that is within. The poems that
describe his entry into winter are not merely about himself as
subject. As he explained in the essay "The Figure of the Youth as
Virile Poet," poetry of necessity is "a process of the personality
of the poet" but with an intended universal application. These
are the "poems of our climate." "America was always North to
him,"[12] a land where God is in hiding.

In the first part of this chapter we will explore this region of
cold as seen in the poems, "The Snow Man," "Evening without
Angels," and "The Emperor of Ice-Cream." In the succeeding
section two very late poems "Not Ideas about the Thing but the
Thing Itself" and "Of Mere Being," written respectively in the
year before and the year of the poet's death, display the hints of
spring with its relief from the cold.

Bare, Bare Is Best

"The Snow Man" is one of the most read of Stevens' poems; it is also the most "over" read. Harold Bloom finds little in it in its almost journalistic style. According to Bloom, the poem seems only to tell us that it is an illusion to believe that the world mirrors back to us our feelings and values, the so-called "pathetic fallacy." Even the feeling of misery itself is just an illusion because all that is there is "nothing." The poem seems to exemplify what Stevens wrote in another place, "disillusion as the last illusion."[13] It asks us to take on "the mind of winter," which, we are to understand, is itself a "fiction."

William Bevis claims that he wrote his book about Stevens which he called *Mind of Winter* out of his puzzlement with "The Snow Man," its nothingness, blankness, poverty and detachment, what he calls "the truly remarkable vacuities in Stevens' work."[14] Stevens, as usual, is evasive about the exact meaning of what he wrote: "I shall explain 'The Snow Man' as an example of the necessity of identifying oneself with reality in order to understand it and enjoy it."[15]

But what is this reality that is being described by the "listener" who listens to the sound of the wind, which at least has some sound, and to the sound of the snow falling, which has no sound? It is a condition of bareness, little sunlight and a few leaves. We are invited to enter into this nothingness, to behold:

Nothing that is not there and the nothing that is.[16]

In this Zen-like experience of the void, the listener is also "nothing." He has learned his nothingness by having been cold "a long time." He himself is made of snow, is the snow man—that is to say, "no man."

This spiritual state is the necessary starting point, not the end point of Stevens' search for God. In the lengthy series of poems under the title, "The Comedian as the Letter C," the protagonist, Crispin, inhabits "a world without imagination," without God. Crispin's journey of self-discovery begins with a similar self-annihilation. Dissolved and annulled:

> The salt hung on his spirit like a frost,
> The dead brine melted in him like a dew
> Of winter, until nothing of himself
> Remained, except some starker, barer self
> In a starker, barer world, in which the sun
> Was not the sun because it never shone...[17]

Bevis sees Stevens following the path of Christian mysticism. The experience of nothing is a purgation of self; this purgation allows a chastened self, and a chastened imagination, to reenter the world with new humility and awe.[18]

Oftentimes a poem like "Evening without Angels" is read as another attack upon supernaturalism and religious visions of life. A closer reading reveals, however, that "Evening without Angels" is another comment upon the "The Snow Man." What is being rejected are romantic and ultimately self-serving projections upon reality. As in traditional Christian meditative practices, there must be the *via purgativa* ("the way of purgation of self") to be passed through and a needed humility acquired before reality can be experienced in all its authentic wonder.

"Evening without Angels" concludes that:

> Bare night is best. Bare earth is best. Bare, bare,...[19]

Stevens once explained that "bare" stands for the ordinary, the commonplace, the ugly, plain reality,[20] what "The Snow Man" describes as the nothing that is, being itself.

In his essay, "The Noble Rider and the Sound of Words," Stevens described poetry's role as "the triumph of contemplation." Because "the real is constantly being engulfed in the unreal,"[21] the poet "must be able to abstract himself and also to abstract reality, which he does by placing it in his imagination."[22] In this way, he concludes, the poet helps people live their lives.[23] In another place he said that poetry "is a purging of the world's poverty and change and evil and death. It is a present perfecting, a satisfaction in the irremediable poverty of life."[24]

"The barrenness that appears is an exposing"[25] Stevens would write much later in one of the late poems that is another rewriting of the empty vision of "The Snow Man." Although he rarely speaks of it directly, the bareness being exposed is also his own. In this regard Helen Vendler calls attention to a telling paragraph in Stevens' essay, "Two or Three Ideas," which expresses in an oblique way the mentality that wrote "The Snow Man":

> Men in general do not create in light and warmth alone. They create in darkness and coldness. They create when they are hopeless, in the midst of antagonisms, when they are wrong, when their powers are no longer subject to their control. They create as the ministers of evil.[26]

Vendler adds, "Anyone wanting an autobiographical statement from this least public of writers can find it in the above passage by substituting for the word 'men' and its subsequent pronouns the pronoun 'I'—a trick that reveals much in Stevens' poetry as well, where 'he' and 'we' are his habitual way of writing about himself while achieving an ironic distance from personal confession."[27]

Of all his chilly visions, none perhaps is chillier than "The Emperor of Ice-Cream." In a scene of the utter banality of everyday living, a corpse is being covered over with a sheet bearing the deceased's own embroidery. Almost obscenely, ice cream is being made and served and flirtations are taking place in the corpse's presence. The horny feet of the dead person protrude from the sheet "to show how cold she is, and dumb":

> Let the lamp affix its beam.
> The only emperor is the emperor of ice-cream.[28]

"The Emperor of Ice-Cream" for a long time was Stevens' favorite poem because of all its resonances.[29] One allusion is to Dante's Satan as depicted in the *Inferno,* an emperor of the realm of grief, protruding from the mid-breast above a field of ice.[30] Is the corpse also that of the poet, the author of the pathetic embroidery on the sheet which cannot cover up his coldness and dumbness? Be that as it may, the aim of the poem is clearly stated:

> Let be be finale of seem.[31]

The poet courageously wishes to penetrate beyond "seem" to the real, whatever that may prove to be. There is no question that Stevens' self-perceived inability to believe in any traditional sense bothered him greatly. It was in great part what his experience of the cold was all about. In the poem "Palace of the Babies," Stevens describes a "disbeliever" walking at night. He can imagine himself succumbing to a vision of a shimmering room full of babies (babies being the little children we must become in the gospel in order to inherit the kingdom of God?). But no such solace is possible for "...in his heart his disbelief lay cold."[32]

At the Earliest Ending of Winter

Wallace Stevens, at the end of his writing life—which is co-extensive with his total life—was graced to see glimpses of winter's retreat. All his poems which make up a single never-ending poem can be truly regarded as evidence of an achieved amassing harmony. Frank Kermode, the British critic, has written that Stevens taught us all not only how to live but how to die in the majestic, serene peacefulness of his last poems. Such peacefulness was born of a profound trust in reality which Stevens came to believe was not misplaced. In the Bible God, after the Flood of destruction, gave a promise to Noah of total fidelity, a promise which is renewed and mirrored in the unchanging succession of the seasons and the faithful succession of day and night.[33] In his long meditative poem "An Ordinary Evening in New Haven," he speaks of morning and evening as being "like promises kept," "this faithfulness of reality." With playful imagery Stevens imagines life's renewal in the shape of the first letter of the alphabet—a baby tottering on unsure legs as he perceives the letter A. Even though the poet is at this point more like the "twisted, stooping, polymathic Z," he perceives that "reality is the beginning not the end":

....Alpha continues to begin.
Omega is refreshed at every end.[34]

The very last poem in *The Collected Poems* is "Not Ideas about the Thing but the Thing Itself." Stevens had resisted Alfred Knopf's suggestion that he publish a collection of all his poems because it seemed to him to be too final. This poem, and one written in 1955 and published only after his death, "Of Mere Being," may be taken as statements of Stevens' point of arrival at the end of his spiritual quest which he conceived to be never-ending and endlessly elaborating. "Abstraction" for Stevens was a method for perceiving the "first idea" of things; at last he was able to find in "the thing itself," "mere being," sufficient indications of the divinity he always sought.

The time within the poem "Not Ideas about the Thing but the Thing Itself" is March, "at the earliest ending of winter," the season of vacancy. Unexpectedly the poet receives a new knowledge of reality even at this very late point. It comes in the odd form of a "scrawny" bird's cry announcing a dawn that has not yet happened but is in the process of taking place. The scrawny bird's note strikes the poet in amusement like that of a chorister "whose c preceded the choir." The event, he insists three times, is not the product of his sleepy imagination: it is something actual, coming from the "outside." And what an outside this is! The tiny bird cry is nothing less than "part of the colossal sun...still far away."[35]

At last in this fresh elevation of reality the light he had been missing during this long winter is being granted him. Only a few scarce images are arranged by the poet in one of his very last poems written on the edge of eternity. "Of Mere Being"[36] comprises a palm tree whose branches move slowly in a wind, a bird, gold-feathered and fire-fangled, and its "foreign song." The decor of the entire scene is of bronze, the bronze of lasting achievement. Horace, the Roman poet, boasted of his poetry in the age of Augustan imperial glory that "I have built a monument more lasting than bronze." Stevens feels something of the same satisfaction, having transcended the despair of "The Emperor of Ice-Cream" where his verses were merely pathetic stitchings upon a burial sheet.

In this austere environment we have come to "the end of the

mind," a region that is strange because it is not human anymore. The palm tree stands at the farthest reach of human thought and "on the edge of space." The bird's song is a "foreign" song, "without human meaning, without human feeling." The poet at last has gone beyond human consolation, beyond what human reason can prove or disclose. But reason in the end is of little account for "you know then that it is not the reason/That makes us happy or unhappy."

The bird with feathers of fire of course evokes the mythical Phoenix, reborn from the flames of its own ashes, the bird of immortality. Because the bird's feathers "dangle down," not upward, commentators have compared it to the pigeons at the end of "Sunday Morning" that sink downward to darkness. For them Stevens, even here at the end, is consistent in his denial of any life beyond what we know. But I would say in response that the song the bird sings is not a human melody: it sings of another realm. Like the bird cry of "Not Ideas," it comes from outside ourselves. The feathers dangle down for the same reason that the pigeons' flight is toward the earth—to link all that we know and are to all that is to be.

Harold Bloom is right when he reads Wallace Stevens as uniquely qualified to write "the poems of our climate." Stevens, according to Bloom, is engaged in a project to replace our native American religion which is a new form of ancient Gnosticism. For the Gnostics, the material universe is a cold chaos that is to be abandoned as the soul takes flight to another realm. It is precisely this chilly vision's inadequacies that these final poems of affirmation highlight and escape.[37]

By coincidence when I was writing the above lines I was spending my mornings back at the seminary in Rome going about my research, and the afternoons, by way of a break, visiting one or another of the many ancient churches. I was greatly taken aback one afternoon when I entered the church of Santa Cecilia in Trastevere and saw a detail of the apse mosaic I had missed on previous occasions. At the extreme left of a majestic depiction of the world to come with Christ at the center was a luxuriant palm tree whose fertile green bespoke the ancient paradise from which we were once expelled but which Christ has now restored to us. I was truly startled to examine the palm tree more closely and discover in its branches a fire-colored bird.

Perhaps it was mere coincidence that this Roman mosaic would so closely depict Stevens' vision of the palm at the end of the mind. But maybe not. Was not Rome for Stevens "the threshold of heaven"?

> ...He stops upon this threshold,
> As if the design of all his words takes form
> And frame from thinking and is realized.[38]

St. Anselm of Canterbury (1033–1109) was a theologian of great accomplishment. His ontological argument for God's existence has many notable flaws as more skeptical thinkers have pointed out. When the skeptics assert that describing a being as "necessary" to the mind does not infer that such a being actually exists, they miss the fact that Anselm truly *knew* God actually, and not merely in his thought, as "necessary." The existence of God was the most fundamental truth of his experience. In Anselm's world view, we should remember, theology was regarded as the "queen of the sciences" because it was based upon divine revelation, the most secure ground of certainty; the empirical sciences, on the other hand, were beneath both theology and philosophy as sources of knowledge because their foundation was merely human observation. Stevens wished to make God's existence "necessary" in the same way, but within a changed world view. Wallace Stevens' use of "necessary" in "The Necessary Angel" is akin to this. It is a fact of experience prior to logic. Anselm lived in a religious age where the existence of God pervaded everything; Stevens did not, and therein lies his great achievement: that he helped people today to find God necessary in the more challenging circumstances of our age.

Both Anselm and Stevens employed "fictions" to communicate ultimate reality. Anselm puts it this way:

No one paints on water or in air, because no traces of the pictures would remain. Now when we present unbelievers with these harmonies you speak of, as so many pictures of a real event, they think that this belief of ours is a fiction *(figmentum)* and not a real happening, so they judge that we are, as it were, painting on a cloud.[39]

Stevens in a letter addressed the problem of explaining what his poems mean. He uses the image of a man walking on the bank of a river whose shadow falls upon the water as he walks. The man walks, the shadow falls, the river moves, much like Anselm's painting on a cloud:

Obviously, it is not possible to tell one what one's own poems mean, or were intended to mean. On the other hand, it is not the simplest thing in the world to explain a poem. I thought of it this way this morning: a poem is like a man walking on the bank of a river, whose shadow is reflected in the water. If you explain a poem, you are quite likely to do it either in terms of the man or in terms of the shadow, but you have to explain it in terms of the whole. When I said recently that a poem was what was on a page, it seems to me now that I was wrong because this is explaining in terms of the man. But the thing and its double always go together.[40]

This ultimately is the irreplaceable function that poetry performs for us: to evoke in speech those harmonies that help us live.

NOTES

[1] L, 348–49.

[2] Alan Filreis, *Wallace Stevens and the Actual World* (Princeton: Princeton University, 1991) 25.

[3] "Adagia," in OP, 187.

[4] "Notes toward a Supreme Fiction," in CP, 404. See Janet McCann, *Wallace Stevens Revisited: The Celestial Possible* (New York: Twayne, 1995) 130.

[5] Harold Bloom, ed., *Wallace Stevens: Modern Critical Views* (New York: Chelsea House, 1985) 12.

[6] "Notes toward a Supreme Fiction," in CP, 404.

[7] Joan Richardson, "Learning Stevens's Language: The Will and the Weather," in *Teaching Wallace Stevens: Practical Essays,* ed. John N. Serio and B.J. Leggett (Knoxville: University of Tennessee, 1994) 140.

[8] "Adagia," in OP, 187.

[9] Ibid., 201.

[10] "Like Decorations in a Nigger Cemetery," in CP, 156.

[11] "Farewell to Florida," in CP, 117–18.

[12] "The Comedian as the Letter C," in CP, 34.

[13] "An Ordinary Evening in New Haven," in CP, 468.

[14] William Bevis, *Mind of Winter: Wallace Stevens, Meditation, and Literature* (Pittsburgh: University of Pittsburgh, 1988) 3.

[15] Ibid., 226.

[16] "The Snow Man," in CP, 10.

[17] "The Comedian as the Letter C," in CP, 29.

[18] William Bevis, *Mind of Winter,* 190.

[19] "Evening without Angels," in CP, 137.

[20] L, 636.

[21] Introduction, in NA, viii.

[22] "The Noble Rider and the Sound of Words" (essay), in NA, 23.

[23] Introduction, in NA, viii; and "The Noble Rider and the Sound of Words" (essay), in NA, 16–23.

[24] "Adagia," in OP, 193.

[25] "An Ordinary Evening in New Haven," in CP, 487.

[26] "Two or Three Ideas" (essay), in OP, 262.

[27] Helen Vendler, "Posthumous Work and Beautiful Subjects," *The New Yorker,* November 12, 1990, 128.

[28] "The Emperor of Ice-Cream," in CP, 64.

[29] Joan Richardson, *Wallace Stevens: A Biography. The Early Years: 1879–1923,* 358 n. 4.

[30] Canto XXXIV.

[31] "The Emperor of Ice-Cream," in CP, 64.

[32] "Palace of the Babies," in CP, 77.

[33] Gn 8:22.

[34] "An Ordinary Evening in New Haven," in CP, 469.

[35] "Not Ideas about the Thing but the Thing Itself," in CP, 534.

[36] "Of Mere Being," in OP, 141.

[37] Harold Bloom, *The American Religion: The Emergence of the Post-Christian Nation* (New York: Simon and Schuster, 1992) 258.

[38] "To an Old Philosopher in Rome," in CP, 511.

[39] Anselm of Canterbury, *Why God Became Man,* I, 4.

[40] L, 354.

5

The Religious Imagination in a Secular Age: Indications for Our Spiritual Life

Once, in a retreat for lawyers and judges, I included a conference on Wallace Stevens. Having been a practicing lawyer himself all his professional life and at the same time having maintained a vibrant spiritual life, Stevens seemed a good model for them in their spiritual strivings. After the conference one of the lawyers approached me with a lawyer-like question. As a married man with children and as a person with a profession, how precisely could Wallace Stevens help him maintain his spiritual life?

I thought I had given some indications, but perhaps I had spent so much time, as a theologian, exploring the hiddenness of God in Stevens' poetry that the spiritual implications of Stevens had escaped him. The poetry also, admittedly, is not the easiest to read.

Here then, in this concluding chapter, are some of the ways I believe Wallace Stevens may continue to be a source of encouragement to people who are trying in their own ways to live spiritually in the discouraging circumstances of today.

His was a genuinely religious imagination that found itself out of place in the secular age in which we have to live and out of place also to an extent with traditional religious forms and expressions. What he experienced can help others live a more authentic religious life of their own.

The Holiness of Ordinary Life

It is a perennial human tendency to confuse the divine with the extraordinary and miraculous, those exceptional moments when God "intervenes" in human affairs. There is beneath this tendency a great alienation—from oneself and from the world we inhabit every day. "Real" life, our true home, is perceived to be somewhere else, literally "out of this world." Sometimes religion itself fosters such confusion and alienation. It was this distortion of religion that Wallace Stevens explicitly rejected. "I am a native in this world / And think in it as a native thinks,"[1] Stevens declares. Somehow God must be found in the ordinary events of everyday life, in "a nice shady home" "and daughters with curls" as Crispin discovered at the end of his journey around the world[2] in the deliberately homely description Stevens chooses. Every day must be miraculous.

"The Man with the Blue Guitar" concludes with the question, "Who are you?" The answer is, "You are yourself," not just on Sunday, but on all the Mondays of your life.[3]

"The joy of having a body,"[4] "the genius of the body, which is our world"[5]—this also must be incorporated into a religious conception of our life. The earth itself must be embraced as our home, Stevens declared: "I call you by name, my green, my fluent mundo."[6] "There is no other world," Stevens explained to Simons. "We live in a world plainly plain. Everything is as you see it."[7]

Although this may be considered pagan and non-Christian, this emphasis upon our earthly existence and body is intended to fill out and correct certain incompletenesses in traditional Christian theology. Augustine was great at explaining the necessity of divine grace to conquer the disordered drives of the human body, but he was not so helpful by downplaying the body as part of our human identity. A whole theology of bodiliness still awaits being taken up, and Wallace Stevens has helped us to see its necessity. After all, the ancient Christian creeds, unlike the philosophy of Plato, cannot even conceive of the afterlife apart from the body and expects the resurrection of the body as essential to human existence.[8]

With so much emphasis in Christianity on the necessity of

redemption for fallen creation, creation itself, its goodness and integrity, has been given insufficient attention. Creation always retains its relationship with God the creator who dwells in "heaven," which is to say, God is not the same as the creation but transcends it. But the kingdom of heaven actually refers to God's rule over the earth, about something happening in this world. Heaven is the future of the earth, not some other realm.[9] These aspects of Christian theology need further elaboration if the full religious significance of our earthly life is to be appreciated and honored.

Maybe, too, like a lot of people, Wallace Stevens felt it was somehow disloyal to find himself closer to God in nature than in churches. But this, again, is to set up a false competition between God's revelation in nature, which necessarily reflects the One who made it, and God's revelation recorded in the scriptures which is its complement. Stevens' desire to find again some groves still sacred enough that Christians had to be warned against frequenting them is an authentic twentieth-century religious person's aspiration to recover the sense of the holy which has been receding everywhere.

Coming from a purely theological perspective, Cardinal Henri de Lubac (1896–1991) made a critique of the museum-like quality of much contemporary religious thought that has many parallels with Stevens. One might say that the theologian and the poet mounted their critiques from a similar religious impulse. According to de Lubac, the ossified scholastic theology of the post-Enlightenment period actually laid the groundwork and was partially responsible for Nietzschean atheism, the "founding rupture," as he called it, of our day. "A right understanding of this relationship (between the natural and the supernatural) permits the problem of modernity to be broached in a non-dualistic way," de Lubac claimed. "The church's capacity to announce Christ to the world depends very much on the idea that one has of nature, in other words, of the created being in its relationship with God as creator and savior."[10]

To create a safe zone for God and grace, beyond the Enlightenment's withering rationalism, theology in recent times

had relegated "nature" to the totally secular realm and constructed a "supernature" as a second or added nature which
human reason could not explain and which was owed to the gra-
tuitous impulse of divine grace. But in the attempt to avoid confusion between what was properly human and what was
distinctly divine, the prevailing theology, in fact, created an omi-
nous separation: of God from the world, of religion from culture.

Such a theology, fabricated to do battle with the
Enlightenment critique of religion, actually bought into the
Enlightenment methodology. These "rationalist" theologians, as
de Lubac described them,

> were somewhat like curators in a museum, a museum in
> which we have inventoried, ordered, and labelled every-
> thing; we know how to define all the terms, we have
> answered all objections, we bring the precise and needed
> distinctions to bear. Everything is obscure there for the pro-
> fane, but for us everything is clear, everything explained. If
> there is still a mystery there, at least we know exactly where
> to place it, and we can point with our fingers to where
> exactly it lies. We are aware of being specialists at knowing
> what the average Christian does not know, just as the spe-
> cialist in chemistry or in trigonometry knows what the
> average student does not know.[11]

Theology, in such a conception, becomes a specialization
related to certain dogmatic "facts" separated from life. Terming
such a theology "shabby," de Lubac asserts that it makes
"dogma a kind of 'superstructure,' believing that, if it is to
remain 'supernatural,' it must be 'superficial' and thinking that
by cutting it off from all human roots, it is making dogma all the
more divine. It is as if God were not the author of both nature
and grace, and of nature in view of grace."[12]

The Love of God

God, seeking God, achieving God, loving God as one's Interior
Paramour, the Supreme Fiction, the One about whom Stevens

wrote, "And for what, except for you, do I feel love?"[13]—the "center" he always sought and never ceased to seek—this was what Wallace Stevens was all about. But the God he sought was not the same as the One he learned about in Sunday school. "I am not an atheist," Stevens once confided in a letter, "but I do not believe in the same God I believed in as a boy."[14] God, the mystery at the heart of existence, in fact, became not less a mystery to him as the years unfolded but always more.

Here again the "case" of Wallace Stevens may be seen as the religious dilemma of many modern believers. Oftentimes the representatives of religious institutions appear to claim to know more about the divine mystery than is truly possible. The role of religion, as Cardinal Ratzinger has written, should be seen as more pointing to the real mysteries at the heart of existence than trying to explain the unexplainable.[15]

What Stevens had, in terms of God, was the experience of his own heart. When the culture is as secular as ours is and when the religious traditions seem weak and unconvincing, God may still be encountered, but more in terms of silence and absence. Writing about "The Spiritual Life in a Secular Age," the Yale philosopher Louis Dupré makes this observation: "If fully lived through, the emptiness of one's own heart may turn into a powerful cry for the One who is not there. It is the contradiction of a simultaneous presence and absence."[16] This seems a fairly adequate description of Stevens himself.

Stevens once called up the definition of God given by Nicholas of Cusa as approximating his own: "the Being whose center is everywhere and whose circumference is nowhere."[17] We have already seen in chapter 3 how Stevens in "Notes toward a Supreme Fiction" drew upon Cusa's notion of "learned ignorance" as the only valid approach to God, and how similar Stevens' use of "fictions" is to Cusa's "symbols" in portraying the divine reality. According to Joseph Carroll, more and more Wallace Stevens came to the philosophical conviction that "the poet's individual fictions derive from and reflect essential imagination—that is, the world-creating mind of God."[18] In similar fashion, Cusa, the "artist's philosopher" of the Renaissance, used the then new artistic device of perspective to explain how the human imagination can capture fragmented perspectives of God as manifested in the universe.[19] Both Cusa and Stevens lived in periods when the sacramental order of the world was breaking down. They both came to recognize that human reason couldn't make much sense of things but that imaginative insight could.

When I visited the tomb of Nicholas of Cusa in the Church of San Pietro in Vinculo in Rome, I was struck by the fact that he, as papal diplomat and bishop, carried on a full public life, like Wallace Stevens, and yet was able to engage in the highest speculations about God. Many have lamented that Cusa did not devote more time to his studies which have proven to be so fruitful even down to our age. His burial stone carries an apt summary of his life's work in terms only of his fascination with God:

> He loved God, feared and honored him.
> Him alone did he serve.
> The promised retribution did not fall upon him.

I feel Cusa and Stevens were kindred spirits. Karl Jaspers' testimony to Cusa includes a summary of the religious world in which he lived, a world that was lost to Stevens but one whose spiritual center Stevens strove to recapture. Jaspers writes:

> Cusanus' world is not the enlightened world of "disenchanted" realities, but a sensual and intellectual world, illumined by the radiance of the supernatural. He did not think that things are "never more than" what we know about them, that there is nothing "behind them," but was led by his unknowing knowledge to unfathomable depths.[20]

Although insurance and the law were Wallace Stevens' profession, poetry was his vocation. It gave shape and purpose to his life. More than that, poetry, as Stevens conceived of it, provides the world with the imaginative enlargement of life which puts it on even a higher plane than philosophy. Poetry puts us in contact with God. In two essays Stevens explains how this is so.

In "The Irrational Element in Poetry," Stevens quotes with approval the thesis of the French Catholic priest Henri Brémond that "one writes poetry to find God."²¹ While Stevens avoids applying the term "mysticism" to poetry because he wishes to remain on the earthly plane, he nonetheless states that "[t]he poet who wishes to contemplate the good in the midst of confusion is like the mystic who wishes to contemplate God in the midst of evil."²² In order to do this, Stevens goes on, poets must "purge themselves before reality...in what they intend to be saintly exercises."²³

"The Irrational Element in Poetry" was written in 1936. Seven years later Stevens returned to this same theme in a paper he delivered at Mount Holyoke College under the title, "The Figure of the Youth as Virile Poet." For this presentation he was helped in his analysis by the notions of Henri Bergson who, like Simone Weil, was in the French Catholic orbit, and who had a great influence on him.²⁴ In this particular paper Stevens is contrasting the respective roles of philosophy and poetry. Having made proper bows in the direction of the eminent Thomist, Jacques Maritain, Stevens expresses his preference for poetry which gives the world something more precious than clear ideas: the imagination of life. With Bergson, Stevens allies the poets with the saints and mystics who achieved personal liberation and exaltation by "achieving God."²⁵

It must have been somewhat startling for the original audiences of these papers to have the poet of such sophistication express himself so candidly about the divine vision of life which was the constant object of his meditations.

Living your life according to the noblest conception you can have of it was Wallace Stevens' ultimate distillation of "how to live, what to do." For him, that noblest conception could only be God.

The Necessity of Prayer

As we saw in the first chapter, Stevens insisted that his young Cuban correspondent José Rodríguez Feo spend more time every

day reading, thinking and especially observing. Poetry, or
"prayer," which was for Stevens an equivalent, is the distillation
of all this hard thought and close observation. The details had to
be accurately seen, the particulars attended to, because, as Stevens
said, poetry arises from the daily necessity to get the world right.

The first thing discovered through prayerful meditation is
that we live in a place that is not our own and, much more, not
ourselves.[26] Because our existence is "hard," prayer becomes the
means whereby we overcome the gap between reality and imagination and, by constructing ourselves, discover ourselves.

Meditation, then, is "the essential exercise"[27] whereby we are
able to detect God's presence in our everyday life and achieve a
life refreshed, the strong exhilaration of "an elixir, an excitation,
a pure power."[28]

To practice prayer described in this way, you must purge
yourself of all your previous preconceptions and mental con-
structs in order to see the world again with total candor, an
immaculate beginning to achieve an immaculate end.[29] You
must also compose yourself, gather yourself together into a state
of heightened attention and, through a long process of waiting,
expose yourself to your deepest longings, as Penelope "composed" herself for the presence of her soul's dearest friend.[30]

Prayer, then, requires that we must "abstract" what Stevens
calls the "first idea" of things before these things became
engulfed by unreality. Meditation sets the imagination in motion
so that it can discover the order, the spirit, the compassionate
love at the heart of reality and that are so difficult to detect.
Reality and imagination, that "construct" which Stevens
described as his own way of seeing things, thus exist, according
to Stevens, in mutual dependence.[31] Imagination must be
anchored in reality lest it go off into space, and reality requires
imagination so that its true nature, which lies beneath the
appearances, may be revealed. This, according to Stevens, is "the
sight of simple seeing" whereby:

> ...We seek
> Nothing beyond reality. Within it,

Everything, the spirit's alchemicana
Included, the spirit that goes roundabout
And through included, not merely the visible,

The solid, but the movable, the moment,
The coming on of feasts and the habits of saints,
The pattern of the heavens and high, night air.[32]

"Everything in everything" was how Nicholas of Cusa amended the early Greek philosopher Anaxagoras' formulation, "Everything is everything." The one bespeaks a mystical intuition of an order, the other a final chaos.[33]

A few months before his death Wallace Stevens wrote two prefaces to a new Bollinger edition of the works of Paul Valéry, the French poet who died in 1945. In it Stevens resonates with the words of Valéry that because the universe is itself the effect of some act, the act of Being itself, "by an act of your own you can rejoin the grand design and undertake the imitation of that which has made all things."[34] Stevens attributed such an achievement to his old professor George Santayana in words which apply best to the one who wrote them. These lines express the conviction that the self he constructed was in ultimate harmony with the very structures of the universe:

Total grandeur of a total edifice,
Chosen by an inquisitor of structures
For himself. He stops upon this threshold,
As if the design of all his words takes form
And frame from thinking and is realized.[35]

Making Up One's Mind about the Church

As "an inquisitor of structures," Wallace Stevens had a natural attraction to the church. He saw the need, as he wrote, in his "rage against chaos" to find comfort in the church's "regulations of the spirit." He liked the traditions and drama of the church's liturgy.

> He preferred the brightness of bells,
> The *mille fiori* of vestments,
> The voice of centuries
> On the priestly gramophones.[36]

"No one believes in the church as an institution more than I do,"[37] Stevens wrote, but maybe, like God, it was all just a confection, fluffy glassware like that Venetian creation called *"mille fiori"* ("a thousand flowers").

I recall in this regard making a personal tour of the backstage spaces of the Metropolitan Opera House in New York City. We passed through the star dressing rooms, the rehearsal rooms, the costume storage, the larger-than-life scenery and the enormous machinery which created the magical illusions and stirred the deepest emotions that are the attraction of the world of the opera. Given this noble enterprise, what struck me backstage mostly was how scruffy it was, the factory-like work areas where carpenters actually made the scenery, the tattered condition of much of the costumery, the scratched painted surfaces of the elevators. Was this all that Stevens' poetry comes down to: the illusion of imagery, or, as Joseph Riddel came to believe, "a world of words to the end of it,"[38] just words?

That frightening possibility occurred to Stevens as well. This is why, as we have seen, he insisted that reality always be the base of his "reality and imagination complex," that they exist together in mutual dependence. Similarly with regard to the church, it, too, had to be part of a "final seriousness."

Two years before his death, Wallace Stevens confessed to his Irish friend Thomas MacGreevy, "At my age, it would be nice to be able to read more and think more and be myself more and to make up my mind about God, say, before it is too late, or at least before he makes up his mind about me."[39] Part of making up his mind about God involved coming to terms finally with the church. Just as the God he came to believe in was not "the sort of God in Whom we were all brought up to believe,"[40] neither, perhaps, would be the form of Christianity he ultimately came to accept. As he described, a chapel suitable for his prayer in "St.

Armorer's Church from the Outside," it would perhaps have to be "underneath" the ruined church above it, closer to the earth.

It bothered Stevens very much that the church as he experienced it with Protestantism had lost much of its vital force. The Lion of Judah in the modern world, he wrote in "An Ordinary Evening in New Haven," has taken on the dimensions of a pet cat;[41] in another poem, the Paraclete has become the parakeet.[42] After visiting a chapel in New York City, Stevens lamented its poverty of symbol, its lack of connection with the Palestinian soil out of which the church originally sprang.[43] In the poem, "Winter Bells," he concedes the need for "regulations of the spirit" but the church, for all its ceremonial beauty, seems more today a custodian of social custom, a haven for the self-satisfied.

> How good life is, on the basis of propriety,
> To be followed by a platter of capon![44]

Helen Vendler has said that Stevens in Hartford, in his search for a good sermon, used to drop in at a local synagogue where the rabbi had the reputation of being a good speaker. In any case, having Wallace Stevens in the congregation would have been quite a challenge for anybody.

The associations of Wallace Stevens with Catholicism were many and warm. French Catholicism, with its intellectual heritage, was a great part of it, as we have seen. He was the generous and faithful correspondent of two unusual nuns, the poet Sister Madeleva and the literary Sister Bernetta Quinn[45] who represented the flourishing state of Catholicism in America in the post-war period. But perhaps the most decisive influence in bringing Stevens to the church was played by more "down-to-earth" persons, such as his associate John Ladish with the Knights of Columbus pin on his lapel, and Arthur Sigmans, another colleague at the Hartford, who with his wife Mary were his godparents at his Catholic baptism.[46]

A priest of the local Passionist monastery in West Hartford, Father Cassian Yuhaus, recalls Stevens' visit to the monastery soon after it was built. He was in the company of Arthur and Mary Sigmans who were active supporters of the monastery. It was

Stevens who insisted upon visiting the chapel.[47] The visit occurred shortly before Stevens' final hospitalization, during which, according to Arthur Sigmans, Stevens was baptized a Catholic.[48]

After Stevens' death, Father Yuhaus kept up a correspondence with Elsie, to provide consolation and also hoping "that she too would be received into the church." He visited the Stevenses' home and prayed with her. Soon, however, Father Yuhaus was transferred by his religious congregation to another monastery and lost contact.

In a letter kept in the archives of the Archdiocese of Hartford, Rev. A.P. Hanley explained in 1986 to the then archbishop how he as hospital chaplain had baptized Stevens but did not record the fact at the instruction of the previous archbishop to avoid "the impression that anyone who came to the hospital would be urged to become a Catholic."

Father Robert Ladish, the son of another of Stevens' co-workers, speculated that it was Monsignor John Burns, the long-time rector of St. Thomas Seminary in the Bloomfield suburb of Hartford, to whom Stevens had turned to receive formal instruction in the Catholic faith. But as for how it was that Stevens was granted "the grace of conversion," as Father Ladish put it, at the end, Ladish felt it had something to do with Stevens' kindness to Elsie to whom he remained faithful and of whom he was protective all their married life. Stevens certainly was a difficult person, arrogant even, certainly elitist. But there was also that very private side which he shared with few and which with some disguises he confided to his poetry. In reading the poems this final turn is not so surprising after all. Let one final poem suffice. It is "Reply to Papini."

Giovanni Papini (1881–1956) was a prolific novelist, poet and critic who, in the disillusionment which followed the First World War, became a Catholic. His *History of Christ,* written in 1921, went into thirty-five editions in Italian alone. A Bergsonian himself, Papini was also sympathetic to American philosophical currents and to William James in particular. The work of Papini to which Stevens makes his "Reply" was a fictional *Letter of Celestin VI, Pope to the Poets.* The pope advises, "Cease, then, from being the astute calligraphers of congealed daydreams, the hunters of cerebral phosphorescences."

Stevens evidently felt this to be a challenge to his very poetic vocation. At the same time it touched a nerve because Stevens himself was constantly aware of the danger of poets becoming unanchored in their own introspections. Stevens replies:

> Is Celestin dislodged? The way through the world
> Is more difficult to find than the way beyond it.[49]

Self-defensively the poem continues:

> ...The poet does not speak in ruins

> Nor stand there making orotund consolations.
> He shares the confusions of intelligence.[50]

Nonetheless the fervent wish of the poet's heart is revealed:

> ...how
> He wishes that all hard poetry were true.[51]

Wallace Stevens wished to be the Dante after Darwin, the religious poet in a non-religious age. He had to deal with all the intellectual reservations of his age and still live in a religious universe. *Refacimento,* "remaking" in Italian, was the original title of "Notes toward a Supreme Fiction." That poem and all the others stand as testimony as to how well he succeeded.

There is in Dante, as well as in Stevens, a homesickness for the earth and a homecoming there as well. Dante's *Commedia,* like Stevens' "Comedian as the Letter C," is a gigantic spiral and journeying of return. They both never leave the ground. Heaven, Purgatory and Hell, as Dante believed, are revealed as they really are: they provide public significance and private substance to our earthly lives. They promise a justice which is more than human. They dramatize the eternal repercussions of the time-bound decisions taken by the obscurest individual. But if, in our post-Darwinian world, the earth is just an old chaos of the sun, or island solitude, then those who would love her are truly "pitiful," as Stevens describes them in the posthumously published poem, "For an Old Woman in a Wig":

> O pitiful lovers of earth, why are you keeping
> Such count of beauty in the ways you wonder?[52]

Judge John Noonan places Stevens among the "Harvard converts" to Catholicism.[53] If this is so, the seeds of that conversion were sown in those formative conversations that the young undergraduate had with the philosopher-poet, George Santayana. It was from Santayana that Stevens absorbed his first lessons in Catholicism, especially its mystical side. But in the end the pupil exceeded the professor in belief.

In his essay, "Understanding, Imagination and Mysticism," Santayana examines the phenomenon of mysticism while safely keeping his distance. The aesthete that Santayana was certainly did not desire "to return to the condition of protoplasm" which is how he describes the mystical state. He writes:

> The way of true wisdom, therefore, if true wisdom is to deal with the Absolute, can only lie in abstention: neither the senses nor the common understanding, and much less the superstructure raised upon these by imagination, logic, or tradition, must delude us....Everything, says the mystic, is nothing, in comparison with the One....The ideal of mysticism is accordingly exactly contrary to the ideal of reason; instead of perfecting human nature it seeks to abolish it...instead of developing our mind to greater scope and precision, it would return to the condition of protoplasm—the blessed consciousness of an Unutterable Reality....The mystical spirit...will never be satisfied...with anything short of Absolute Nothing.[54]

William Bevis considers these views of Santayana less an explanation of the mystical phenomenon than an attack upon it. Santayana, the aesthete, Bevis ironically comments, "somehow in transition to Cambridge had lost sympathy with the visions of Castile."[55] Castile refers of course to the great Spanish mystics Teresa of Avila and John of the Cross.

First of all, according to Bevis, the "nothing" that mystics find is not a value judgment leveled against everything else but a true experience of the Nameless One: it is of the essence of the mystical experience. Over against such fanaticism, Santayana proposes a "partial" mysticism to bring out "with wonderful intensity" some basic layers of human experience. "[M]oderately indulged in and duly inhabited by a residuum of conventional sanity," Santayana continues, "it serves to give a touch of strangeness and elevation to the character." On this Bevis wryly concludes, "That sort of most scrutable thinking, not the inscrutable East, later created a multimillion dollar American industry in transcendental meditation, and apparently became a Panglossian Harvard convention."[56]

Bevis then compares Stevens to his mentor: "Stevens repeatedly proposes a different scenario, more respectful of meditation but also in some ways Christian: the experience of nothing is a purgation of self; this purgation allows a chastened self, and a chastened imagination, to reenter the world with new humility and wonder. Thus even in poems we might not call meditative, Stevens' knowledge of 'bare' states of mind helped structure his thought."[57]

Perhaps to some of his more sophisticated admirers Wallace Stevens' entry into the Catholic Church may seem unthinkable still. A St. Christopher medal was pinned to the pillow on which his head rested in his casket. I think Wallace Stevens would have found this touch delightful.

[1] "The Man with the Blue Guitar," in CP, 180.

[2] "The Comedian as the Letter C," in CP, 40, 43.

[3] "The Man with the Blue Guitar," in CP, 183.

[4] "Evening without Angels," in CP, 136.

[5] "Esthétique du Mal," in CP, 317.

[6] "Notes toward a Supreme Fiction," in CP, 407.

[7] Cited by Robert Rehder, *The Poetry of Wallace Stevens* (New York: Macmillan, 1988) 175.

[8] Margaret R. Miles, *Desire and Delight: A New Reading of St. Augustine's Confessions* (New York: Crossroad, 1992) 98–99.

[9] See Joseph Ratzinger, *Eschatology, Death and Eternal Life* (Washington, D.C.: Catholic University of America, 1988) 26: "The affirmation that 'the kingdom of God is at hand' can be paraphrased 'God is close.' First and foremost Jesus is not speaking of a heavenly reality but of something God is doing and will do in the future here in earth."

[10] See Georges Chartraine, "Cardinal Henri de Lubac," *Communio* 18 (Fall 1991): 302–3.

[11] "Causes internes de l'attenuation et de la disparition du sens du Sacré," in *Théologie dans l'histoire: II* (Paris: Desclée de Brouwer, 1990) 23.

[12] Cited by Joseph A. Komonchak, "Theology and Culture at Mid-Century: The Example of Henri de Lubac," *Theological Studies* 51 (December 1990): 582.

[13] "Notes toward a Supreme Fiction," in CP, 380.

[14] L, 735.

[15] See Joseph Ratzinger's critique of *Gaudium et spes,* which contains the first treatment ever by an ecumenical council of the phenomenon of atheism, in *Commentary on the Documents of Vatican II,* ed. Herbert Vorgrimler (New York: Crossroad, 1989) 5:155.

[16] Louis Dupré, "Spiritual Life in a Secular Age," *Daedalus* 3 (1982) 25.

[17] "A Collect of Philosophy" (essay), in OP, 275. Stevens incorrectly attributes this definition to Blaise Pascal. See two works by Jasper Hopkins, *Nicholas of Cusa's Dialectical Mysticism: Text, translation and interpretative study of "De visione Dei"* (Minneapolis: Arthur J. Banning, 2nd ed., 1988) 129–30; and *A*

Concise Introduction to the Philosophy of Nicholas of Cusa (Minneapolis: University of Minnesota, 1986) 149.

[18] Joseph Carroll, *Wallace Stevens' Supreme Fiction: A New Romanticism* (Baton Rouge: Louisiana State, 1987) 260.

[19] Ronald Levao, *Renaissance Minds: Cusanus, Signey, Shakespeare* (Berkeley: University of California, 1985) 85.

[20] Karl Jaspers, *Anselm and Nicholas of Cusa* (New York: Harcourt, Brace, Jovanovich, 1974) 175.

[21] "The Irrational Element in Poetry" (essay), in OP, 226.

[22] Ibid., 230.

[23] Ibid., 231.

[24] See Joseph N. Riddel, *The Clairvoyant Eye: The Poetry and Poetics of Wallace Stevens* (Baton Rouge: Louisiana State, 1965) 37–38, 39, 271–74.

[25] "The Figure of the Youth as Virile Poet" (essay), in NA, 51.

[26] "Notes toward a Supreme Fiction," in CP, 383.

[27] "The World as Meditation," in OP, 520.

[28] "Notes toward a Supreme Fiction," in CP, 382.

[29] Ibid., 382

[30] "The World as Meditation," in CP, 521.

[31] "Notes toward a Supreme Fiction," in CP, 392.

[32] "An Ordinary Evening in New Haven," in CP, 471–72.

[33] See Justus George Lawler, *Celestial Pantomime: Poetic Structures of Transcendence* (New Haven: Yale, 1979) 207.

[34] Paul Valéry, *Dialogues,* trans. William McCausland Stewart, with two prefaces by Wallace Stevens (New York: Pantheon Books, Bollinger Series XLV. 4, 1956) xiii.

[35] "To an Old Philosopher in Rome," in CP, 510–11.

[36] "Winter Bells," in CP, 141.

[37] L, 348

[38] Riddel, *The Clairvoyant Eye,* 285.

[39] L, 763.

[40] L, 348.

[41] "An Ordinary Evening in New Haven," in CP, 472–73.

[42] "The Bird with the Coppery, Keen Claws," in CP, 82.

[43] L, 140.

[44] "Winter Bells," in CP, 141.

[45] In an unpublished essay, Maureen Kravec speculates that since Stevens did not have an easy time relating to women, his being able to establish nonthreatening, pleasant friendships with the two nuns might have helped Stevens reconcile himself to the feminine.

[46] Interview by the author with Fr. John Ladish, April 12, 1993.

[47] Interview by the author with Fr. Cassian Yuhaus C.P., St. Gabriel's Convent, Clarks Summit, Pa., June 28, 1993.

[48] Peter Brazeau, *Parts of a World: Wallace Stevens Remembered. A Oral Biography* (New York: Random House, 1983) 290.

[49] "Reply to Papini," in CP, 446.

[50] Ibid., 446.

[51] Ibid., 447.

[52] "For an Old Woman in a Wig," in OP, 20.

[53] John Noonan, "The Catholic Community at Harvard," *New Oxford Review* 59 (March 1992): 6.

[54] Cited by William M. Bevis, *Mind of Winter: Wallace Stevens, Meditation and Literature* (Pittsburgh: University of Pittsburgh, 1988) 226.

[55] Ibid., 189.

[56] Ibid., 188.

[57] Ibid., 190.

Part Two
The Poetry

TO AN OLD PHILOSOPHER IN ROME

On the threshold of heaven, the figures in the street
Become the figures of heaven, the majestic movement
Of men growing small in the distances of space,
Singing, with smaller and still smaller sound,
Unintelligible absolution and an end—

The threshold, Rome, and the more merciful Rome
Beyond, the two alike in the make of the mind.
It is as if in a human dignity
Two parallels become one, a perspective, of which
Men are part both in the inch and in the mile.

How easily the blown banners change to wings...
Things dark on the horizons of perception,
Become accompaniments of fortune, but
Of the fortune of the spirit, beyond the eye,
Not of its sphere, and yet not far beyond,

The human end in the spirit's greatest reach,
The extreme of the known in the presence of the extreme
Of the unknown. The newsboys' muttering
Becomes another murmuring; the smell
Of medicine, a fragrantness not to be spoiled...

The bed, the books, the chair, the moving nuns,
The candle as it evades the sight, these are
The sources of happiness in the shape of Rome,
A shape within the ancient circles of shapes,
And these beneath the shadow of a shape

In a confusion on bed and books, a portent
On the chair, a moving transparence on the nuns,
A light on the candle tearing against the wick
To join a hovering excellence, to escape
From fire and be part only of that of which

Fire is the symbol: the celestial possible.
Speak to your pillow as if it was yourself.
Be orator but with an accurate tongue
And without eloquence, O, half-asleep,
Of the pity that is the memorial of this room,

So that we feel, in this illumined large,
The veritable small, so that each of us
Beholds himself in you, and hears his voice
In yours, master and commiserable man,
Intent on your particles of nether-do,

Your dozing in the depths of wakefulness,
In the warmth of your bed, at the edge of your chair, alive
Yet living in two worlds, impenitent
As to one, and, as to one, most penitent,
Impatient for the grandeur that you need

In so much misery; and yet finding it
Only in misery, the afflatus of ruin,
Profound poetry of the poor and of the dead,
As in the last drop of the deepest blood,
As it falls from the heart and lies there to be seen,

Even as the blood of an empire, it might be,
For a citizen of heaven though still of Rome.
It is poverty's speech that seeks us out the most.
It is older than the oldest speech of Rome.
This is the tragic accent of the scene.

And you—it is you that speak it, without speech,
The loftiest syllables among loftiest things,
The one invulnerable man among
Crude captains, the naked majesty, if you like,
Of bird-nest arches and of rain-stained-vaults.

The sounds drift in. The buildings are remembered,
The life of the city never lets go, nor do you
Ever want it to. It is part of the life in your room.

Its domes are the architecture of your bed.
The bells keep on repeating solemn names

In choruses and choirs of choruses,
Unwilling that mercy should be a mystery
Of silence, that any solitude of sense
Should give you more than their peculiar chords
And reverberations clinging to whisper still.

It is a kind of total grandeur at the end,
With every visible thing enlarged and yet
No more than a bed, a chair and moving nuns,
The immensest theatre, the pillared porch,
The book and candle in your ambered room,

Total grandeur of a total edifice,
Chosen by an inquisitor of structures
For himself. He stops upon this threshold,
As if the design of all his words takes form
And frame from thinking and is realized.

THE WORLD AS MEDITATION

> *J'ai passé trop de temps à*
> *travailler mon violon, à voyager.*
> *Mais l'exercice essentiel du*
> *compositeur—la méditation—rien ne*
> *l'a jamais suspendu en moi...Je*
> *vis un rêve permanent, qui ne*
> *s'arrête ni nuit ni jour.*
>
> Georges Enesco

Is it Ulysses that approaches from the east,
The interminable adventurer? The trees are mended.
That winter is washed away. Someone is moving

On the horizon and lifting himself up above it.
A form of fire approaches the cretonnes of Penelope,
Whose mere savage presence awakens the world in which
      she dwells.

She has composed, so long, a self with which to welcome him,
Companion to his self for her, which she imagined,
Two in a deep-founded sheltering, friend and dear friend.

The trees had been mended, as an essential exercise
In an inhuman meditation, larger than her own.
No winds like dogs watched over her at night.

She wanted nothing he could not bring her by coming
      alone.
She wanted no fetchings. His arms would be her necklace
And her belt, the final fortune of their desire.

But was it Ulysses? Or was it only the warmth of the sun
On her pillow? The thought kept beating in her like her
      heart.
The two kept beating together. It was only day.

It was Ulysses and it was not. Yet they had met,
Friend and dear friend and a planet's encouragement.
The barbarous strength within her would never fail.

She would talk a little to herself as she combed her hair,
Repeating his name with its patient syllables,
Never forgetting him that kept coming constantly so near.

SUNDAY MORNING

I

Complacencies of the peignoir, and late
Coffee and oranges in a sunny chair,
And the green freedom of a cockatoo
Upon a rug mingle to dissipate
The holy hush of ancient sacrifice.
She dreams a little, and she feels the dark
Encroachment of that old catastrophe,
As a calm darkens among water-lights.
The pungent oranges and bright, green wings
Seem things in some procession of the dead,
Winding across wide water, without sound.
The day is like wide water, without sound,
Stilled for the passing of her dreaming feet
Over the seas, to silent Palestine,
Dominion of the blood and sepulchre.

II

Why should she give her bounty to the dead?
What is divinity if it can come
Only in silent shadows and in dreams?
Shall she not find in comforts of the sun,
In pungent fruit and bright, green wings, or else
In any balm or beauty of the earth,
Things to be cherished like the thought of heaven?
Divinity must live with herself:
Passions of rain, or moods in falling snow;
Grievings in loneliness, or unsubdued
Elations when the forest blooms; gusty
Emotions on wet roads on autumn nights;
All pleasures and all pains, remembering
The bough of summer and the winter branch.
These are the measures destined for her soul.

III

Jove in the clouds had his inhuman birth.
No mother suckled him, no sweet land gave
Large-mannered motions to his mythy mind
He moved among us, as a muttering king,
Magnificent, would move among his hinds,
Until our blood, commingling, virginal,
With heaven, brought such requital to desire
The very hinds discerned it, in a star.
Shall our blood fail? Or shall it come to be
The blood of paradise? And shall the earth
Seen all of paradise that we shall know?
The sky will be much friendlier then than now,
A part of labor and a part of pain,
And next in glory to enduring love,
Not this dividing and indifferent blue.

IV

She says, "I am content when wakened birds,
Before they fly, test the reality
Of misty fields, by their sweet questionings;
But when the birds are gone, and their warm fields
Return no more, where, then, is paradise?"
There is not any haunt of prophecy,
Nor any old chimera of the grave,
Neither the golden underground, nor isle
Melodious, where spirits gat them home,
Nor visionary south, nor cloudy palm
Remote on heaven's hill, that has endured
As April's green endures; or will endure
Like her remembrance of awakened birds,
Or her desire for June and evening, tipped
By the consummation of the swallow's wings.

V

She says, "But in contentment I still feel
The need of some imperishable bliss."
Death is the mother of beauty; hence from her,

Alone, shall come fulfillment to our dreams
And our desires. Although she strews the leaves
Of sure obliteration on our paths,
The path sick sorrow took, the many paths
Where triumph rang its brassy phrase, or love
Whispered a little out of tenderness,
She makes the willow shiver in the sun
For maidens who were wont to sit and gaze
Upon the grass, relinquished to their feet.
She causes boys to pile new plums and pears
On disregarded plate. The maidens taste
And stray impassioned in the littering leaves.

VI

Is there no change of death in paradise?
Does ripe fruit never fall? Or do the boughs
Hang always heavy in that perfect sky,
Unchanging, yet so like our perishing earth,
With rivers like our own that seek for seas
They never find, the same receding shores
That never touch with inarticulate pang?
Why set the pear upon those river-banks?
Or spice the shores with odors of the plum?
Alas, that they should wear our colors there,
The silken weavings of our afternoons,
And pick the strings of our insipid lutes!
Death is the mother of beauty, mystical,
Within whose burning bosom we devise
Our earthly mothers waiting, sleeplessly.

VII

Supple and turbulent, a ring of men
Shall chant in orgy on a summer morn
Their boisterous devotion to the sun,
Not as a god, but as a god might be,
Naked among them, like a savage source.
Their chant shall be a chant of paradise,
Out of their blood, returning to the sky;

And in their chant shall enter, voice by voice,
The windy lake wherein their lord delights,
The trees, like serafin, and echoing hills,
That choir among themselves long afterward.
They shall know well the heavenly fellowship
Of men that perish and of summer morn.
And whence they came and whither they shall go
The dew upon their feet shall manifest.

VIII

She hears, upon that water without sound,
A voice that cries, "The tomb in Palestine
Is not the porch of spirits lingering.
It is the grave of Jesus, where he lay."
We live in an old chaos of the sun,
Or old dependency of day and night,
Or island solitude, unsponsored, free,
Of that wide water, inescapable.
Deer walk upon our mountains, and the quail
Whistle about us their spontaneous cries;
Sweet berries ripen in the wilderness;
and, in the isolation of the sky,
At evening, casual flocks of pigeons make
Ambiguous undulations as they sink,
Downward to darkness, on extended wings.

ANGEL SURROUNDED BY PAYSANS

One of the countrymen:
                                     There is
A welcome at the door to which no one comes?
The angel:
      I am the angel of reality,
      Seen for a moment standing in the door.

      I have neither ashen wing nor wear of ore
      And live without a tepid aureole,

      Or stars that follow me, not to attend,
      But, of my being and its knowing, part.

      I am one of you and being one of you
      Is being and knowing what I am and know.

      Yet I am the necessary angel of earth,
      Since, in my sight, you see the earth again,

      Cleared of its stiff and stubborn, man-locked set,
      And, in my hearing, you hear its tragic drone

      Rise liquidly in liquid lingerings,
      Like watery words awash; like meanings said

      By repetitions of half-meanings. Am I not,
      Myself, only half of a figure of a sort,

      A figure half seen, or seen for a moment, a man
      Of the mind, an apparition apparelled in

      Apparels of such lightest look that a turn
      Of my shoulder and quickly, too quickly, I am gone?

ST. ARMORER'S CHURCH FROM THE OUTSIDE

St. Armorer's was once an immense success.
It rose loftily and stood massively; and to lie
In its church-yard, in the province of St. Armorer's,
Fixed one for good in geranium-colored day.

What is left has the foreign smell of plaster,
The closed-in smell of hay. A sumac grows
On the altar, growing toward the lights, inside.
Reverberations leak and lack among holes...

Its chapel rises from Terre Ensevelie,
An ember yes among its cindery noes,
His own: a chapel of breath, an appearance made
For a sign of meaning in the meaningless,

No radiance of dead blaze, but something seen
In a mystic eye, no sign of life but life,
Itself, the presence of the intelligible
In that which is created as its symbol.

It is like a new account of everything old,
Matisse at Vence and a great deal more than that,
A new-colored sun, say, that will soon change forms
And spread hallucinations on every leaf.

The chapel rises, his own, his period,
A civilization formed from the outward blank,
A sacred syllable rising from sacked speech,
The first car out of a tunnel en voyage

Into lands of ruddy-ruby fruits, achieved
Not merely desired, for sale, and market things
That press, strong peasants in a peasant world,
Their purports to a final seriousness—

Final for him, the acceptance of such prose,
Time's given perfections made to seem like less

Than the need of each generation to be itself,
The need to be actual and as it is.

St. Armorer's has nothing of this present,
This *vif,* this dizzle-dazzle of being new
And of becoming, for which the chapel spreads out
Its arches in its vivid element,

In the air of newness of that element,
In an air of freshness, clearness, greenness, blueness,
That which is always beginning because it is part
Of that which is always beginning, over and over.

The chapel underneath St. Armorer's walls,
Stands in a light, its natural light and day.
The origin and keep of its health and his own.
And there he walks and does as he lives and likes.

THE MOTIVE FOR METAPHOR

You like it under the trees in autumn,
Because everything is half dead.
The wind moves like a cripple among the leaves
And repeats words without meaning.

In the same way, you were happy in spring,
With the half colors of quarter-things,
The slightly brighter sky, the melting clouds,
The single bird, the obscure moon—

The obscure moon lighting an obscure world
Of things that would never be quite expressed,
Where you yourself were never quite yourself
And did not want nor have to be,

Desiring the exhilarations of changes:
The motive for metaphor, shrinking from
The weight of primary noon,
The A B C of being,

The ruddy temper, the hammer
Of red and blue, the hard sound—
Steel against intimation—the sharp flash,
The vital, arrogant, fatal, dominant X.

FINAL SOLILOQUY OF THE INTERIOR
PARAMOUR

Light the first light of evening, as in a room
In which we rest and, for small reason, think
The world imagined is the ultimate good.

This is, therefore, the intensest rendezvous.
It is in that thought that we collect ourselves,
Out of all the indifferences, into one thing:

Within a single thing, a single shawl
Wrapped tightly round us, since we are poor, a warmth,
A light, a power, the miraculous influence.

Here, now, we forget each other and ourselves.
We feel the obscurity of an order, a whole,
A knowledge, that which arranged the rendezvous.

Within its vital boundary, in the mind.
We say God and the imagination are one...
How high that highest candle lights the dark.

Out of this same light, out of the central mind,
We make a dwelling in the evening air,
In which being there together is enough.

THE SNOW MAN

One must have a mind of winter
To regard the frost and the boughs
Of the pine-trees crusted with snow;

And have been cold a long time
To behold the junipers shagged with ice,
The spruces rough in the distant glitter

Of the January sun; and not to think
Of any misery in the sound of the wind,
In the sound of a few leaves,

Which is the sound of the land
Full of the same wind
That is blowing in the same bare place

For the listener, who listens in the snow,
And, nothing himself, beholds
Nothing that is not there and the nothing that is.

EVENING WITHOUT ANGELS

> *the great interests of man: air
> and light, the joy of having a
> body, the voluptuousness of
> looking.*
>
> Mario Rossi

Why seraphim like lutanists arranged
Above the trees? And why the poet as
Eternal *chef d'orchestre?*

                Air is air,
Its vacancy glitters round us everywhere.
Its sounds are not angelic syllables
But our unfashioned spirits realized
More sharply in more furious selves.

                And light
That fosters seraphim and is to them
Coiffeur of haloes, fecund jeweller—
Was the sun concoct for angels or for men?
Sad men made angels of the sun, and of
The moon they made their own attendant ghosts,
Which led them back to angels, after death.

Let this be clear that we are men of sun
And men of day and never of pointed night,
Men that repeat antiquest sounds of air
In an accord of repetitions. Yet,
If we repeat, it is because the wind
Encircling us, speaks always with our speech.

Light, too, encrusts us making visible
The motions of the mind and giving form
To moodiest nothings, as, desire for day
Accomplished in the immensely flashing East,
Desire for rest, in that descending sea
Of dark, which in its very darkening
Is rest and silence spreading into sleep.

...Evening, when the measure skips a beat
And then another, one by one, and all
To a seething minor swiftly modulate.
Bare night is best. Bare earth is best. Bare, bare,
Except for our own houses, huddled low
Beneath the arches and their spangled air,
Beneath the rhapsodies of fire and fire,
Where the voice that is in us makes a true response,
Where the voice that is great within us rises up,
As we stand gazing at the rounded moon.

THE EMPEROR OF ICE-CREAM

Call the roller of big cigars,
The muscular one, and bid him whip
In kitchen cups concupiscent curds.
Let the wenches dawdle in such dress
As they are used to wear, and let the boys
Bring flowers in last month's newspapers.
Let be be finale of seem.
The only emperor is the emperor of ice-cream.

Take from the dresser of deal.
Lacking the three glass knobs, that sheet
On which she embroidered fantails once
And spread it so as to cover her face.
If her horny feet protrude, they come
To show how cold she is, and dumb.
Let the lamp affix its beam.
The only emperor is the emperor of ice-cream.

NOT IDEAS ABOUT THE THING
BUT THE THING ITSELF

At the earliest ending of winter,
In March, a scrawny cry from outside
Seemed like a sound in his mind.

He knew that he heard it,
A bird's cry, at daylight or before,
In the early March wind.

The sun was rising at six,
No longer a battered panache above snow...
It would have been outside.

It was not from the vast ventriloquism
Of sleep's faded papier-mâché...
The sun was coming from outside.

That scrawny cry—it was
A chorister whose c preceded the choir.
It was part of the colossal sun,

Surrounded by its choral rings,
Still far away. It was like
A new knowledge of reality.

OF MERE BEING

The palm at the end of the mind,
Beyond the last thought, rises
In the bronze decor,

A gold-feathered bird
Sings in the palm, without human meaning,
Without human feeling, a foreign song.

You know then that it is not the reason
That makes us happy or unhappy.
The bird sings. Its feathers shine.

The palm stands on the edge of space.
The wind moves slowly in the branches.
The bird's fire-fangled feathers dangle down.

REPLY TO PAPINI

> *In all the solemn moments of human*
> *history...poets rose to sing the*
> *hymn of victory or the psalm of*
> *supplication....Cease, then,*
> *from being the astute calligraphers*
> *of congealed daydreams, the hunters*
> *of cerebral phosphorescences.*
>> Letter of Celestin VI, Pope,
>> to the Poets
>> P.C.C. Giovanni Papini

I

Poor procurator, why do you ask someone else
To say what Celestin should say for himself?

He has an ever-living subject. The poet
Has only the formulations of midnight.

Is Celestin dislodged? The way through the world
Is more difficult to find than the way beyond it.

You know that the nucleus of a time is not
The poet but the poem, the growth of the mind

Of the world, the heroic effort to live expressed
As victory. The poet does not speak in ruins

Nor stand there making orotund consolations.
He shares the confusions of intelligence.

Giovanni Papini, by your faith, know how
He wishes that all hard poetry were true.

This pastoral of endurance and of death
Is of a nature that must be perceived

And not imagined. The removes must give,
Including the removes toward poetry.

II

Celestin, the generous, the civilized,
Will understand what it is to understand.

The world is still profound and in its depths
Man sits and studies silence and himself,

Abiding the reverberations in the vaults.
Now, once, he accumulates himself and time

For humane triumphals. But a politics
Of property is not an area

For triumphals. These are hymns appropriate to
The complexities of the world, when apprehended,

The intricacies of appearance, when perceived.
They become our gradual possession. The poet

Increases the aspects of experience,
As in an enchantment, analyzed and fixed

And final. This is the centre. The poet is
The angry day-son clanging at its make:

The satisfaction underneath the sense,
The conception sparkling in still obstinate thought.

Bibliography

WORKS BY WALLACE STEVENS

POETRY AND PLAYS

The Collected Poems. New York: Alfred A. Knopf, 1954. Reprint, New York: Random House, Vintage Books, 1990.

Opus Posthumous: Poems, Plays, Prose. Rev. ed. Edited by Milton J. Bates. New York: Alfred A. Knopf, 1989. Reprint, New York: Random House, Vintage Books, 1990.

The Palm at the End of the Mind: Selected Poems and a Play by Wallace Stevens. Edited by Holly Stevens. New York: Alfred A. Knopf, 1972.

Souvenirs and Prophecies: The Young Wallace Stevens. Edited by Holly Stevens. New York: Alfred A. Knopf, 1977.

PROSE

The Necessary Angel: Essays on Reality and the Imagination. New York: Alfred A. Knopf, 1951. Reprint, New York: Random House, Vintage Books, 1965.

Letters of Wallace Stevens. Edited by Holly Stevens. New York: Alfred A. Knopf, 1966.

Sur Plusieurs Beaux Sujects: Wallace Stevens' Commonplace Book, a Facsimile and Transcription. Edited by Milton J. Bates. Stanford: Stanford University, 1989.

THE LIFE OF WALLACE STEVENS

Brazeau, Peter. *Parts of a World: Wallace Stevens Remembered. An Oral Biography.* New York: Random House, 1983.

Richardson, Joan. *Wallace Stevens: A Biography. The Early Years: 1879–1923.* New York: William Morrow, 1986.

___. *Wallace Stevens: A Biography. The Later Years: 1923–1955.* New York: William Morrow, 1988.

WORKS ABOUT STEVENS' POETRY

Baird, James. *The Dome and the Rock: Structure in the Poetry of Wallace Stevens.* Baltimore: Johns Hopkins University, 1968

Bates, Milton J. *Wallace Stevens: A Mythology of Self.* Berkeley: University of California, 1985.

Beckett, Lucy. *Wallace Stevens.* London: Cambridge University, 1974.

Bevis, William W. *Mind of Winter: Wallace Stevens, Meditation, and Literature.* Pittsburgh: University of Pittsburgh, 1988.

Bloom, Harold. *Wallace Stevens: Modern Critical Views.* New York: Chelsea House, 1985.

___. *Wallace Stevens: The Poems of Our Climate.* Ithaca: Cornell University, 1977.

Brogan, Jacqueline Vaught. *Stevens and Simile: A Theory of Language.* Princeton: Princeton University, 1986.

Brown, Ashley, and Robert S. Haller. *The Achievement of Wallace Stevens: A Critical Anthology.* Philadelphia: J.B. Lippincott, 1962.

Carroll, Joseph. *Wallace Stevens's Supreme Fiction: A New Romanticism.* Baton Rouge: Louisiana State University, 1987.

Filreis, Alan. *Wallace Stevens and the Actual World*. Princeton: Princeton University, 1991.

Fisher, Barbara M. *Wallace Stevens: The Intensest Rendezvous*. Charlottesville: University of Virginia, 1990.

Grey, Thomas C. *The Wallace Stevens Case: Law and the Practice of Poetry*. Cambridge: Harvard University, 1991.

Halliday, Mark. *Stevens and the Interpersonal*. Princeton: Princeton University, 1991.

Jarraway, David R. *Wallace Stevens and the Question of Belief: The Metaphysician in the Dark*. Baton Rouge: Louisiana State University, 1993.

Kermode, Frank. *Wallace Stevens*. London: Faber and Faber, 1989.

La Guardia, David. *Advance on Chaos: The Sanctifying Imagination of Stevens*. Hanover: University Press of New England, 1983.

Leonard, J.S., and C.E. Wharton, *The Fluent Mundo: Wallace Stevens and the Structure of Reality*. Athens: University of Georgia, 1988.

Lensing, Georges. *Wallace Stevens: A Poet's Growth*. Baton Rouge: Louisiana State University, 1986.

Longenback, James. *Wallace Stevens: The Plain Sense of Things*. New York: Oxford University, 1991.

McCann, Janet. *Wallace Stevens Revisited: The Celestial Possible*. New York: Twayne Publishers, 1995.

Morris, Adalaide Kirby. *Wallace Stevens: Imagination and Faith*. Princeton: Princeton University, 1974.

Morse, Samuel French. *Wallace Stevens: Poetry as Life*. New York: Pegasus, 1970.

O'Connor, William Van. *The Shaping Spirit: A Study of Wallace Stevens.* Chicago: Henry Regnery Company, 1950.

Pack, Robert. *Wallace Stevens: An Approach to His Poetry and Thought.* New Brunswick: Rutgers University, 1958.

Penso, Kia. *Wallace Stevens: Harmonium and the Whole of Harmonium.* Hamden: Archon Books, 1991.

Rehder, Robert. *The Poetry of Wallace Stevens.* New York: Macmillan, 1988.

Riddel, Joseph N. *The Clairvoyant Eye: The Poetry and Poetics of Wallace Stevens.* Baton Rouge: Lousisiana State University, 1965.

Schaum, Melita. *Wallace Stevens and the Critical Schools.* Tuscaloosa: University of Alabama, 1988.

Serio, John N., and B.J. Leggett, eds. *Teaching Wallace Stevens: Practical Essays.* Knoxville: University of Tennessee, 1994.

Sukenick, Ronald. *Wallace Stevens: Musing the Obscure.* New York: New York University, 1966.

Vendler, Helen. *On Extended Wings: Wallace Stevens's Longer Poems.* Cambridge: Harvard University, 1969.

___. *Wallace Stevens: Words Chosen Out of Desire.* Knoxville: University of Tennessee, 1984.
Walker, David. *The Transparent Lyric: Reading and Meaning in the Poetry of Stevens and Williams.* Princeton: Princeton University, 1984.

WORKS WHICH TOUCH ON THE ISSUE OF BELIEF IN STEVENS

Abrams, M.H., ed. *Literature and Belief: English Institute Essays, 1957.* New York: Columbia University, 1958.

Donoghue, Denis. *Connoisseurs of Chaos: Ideas of Order in Modern American Poetry*. New York: Columbia University, 1984.

Lawler, Justus George. *Celestial Pantomime: Poetic Structures of Transcendence*. New Haven: Yale University, 1979.